G000061335

~Turkey

1

THE TURKISH KITCHEN

COLOPHON

Editors & Food
Aynur Doğan
Sander Schroevers

Editorial Board
Anda Schippers

Art Director/design
Mathieu Westerveld

Photography
Food4eyes.com
Remco Lassche
Freek Stoltenborgh
Claire Eversdijk
Shoot Studio

Photography Food
Thea Spierings

Styling
Lize Boer

Printer
Vivapress

Assistant editor
Josje Kets

Editor
Pieter Harts

Many thanks to
Subba Nijmegen
Turks verkeersbureau

© English edition 2008
e-mail: info@miller-books.com
www.miller-books.com

© Visconti 2008
ISBN 978 90 8724 097 4

No part of this book may be reproduced in any form or by any electronic or mechanical means, including information storage or retrieval devices or systems, without prior written permission from the publisher.

2

Introduction

The aroma of aubergines grilled on a charcoal fire, the taste of filled wine leaves in olive oil and the wonderful bread...this is what characterises the Turkish kitchen. But just as important for the Turkish eating culture is the ambiance of Mediterranean recreation. You could call it the relaxed dining atmosphere that existed long before relaxed dining became hip: the removal of uncomfortable shoes before taking your seat on cushions and enjoying the lovely first courses (meze) of the raki-table.

The popularity of Turkish cooking is enjoying steady growth, partly due to the thousands of Britons who visit Turkey every year. The health value of the dishes is another reason: many meals contain a lot of fruit and vegetables. Finally, the ingredients are relatively well known; after all, Turkey forms the bridge between Europe and Asia.

In this book, Turkish breakfast, lunch, dinner and party foods are presented in more than seventy authentic and exceptional recipes. Next to the recipes are handy cooking tips and interesting information. In addition, this book teaches you which ingredients to select in Turkish shops so that you can bring that unique Mediterranean atmosphere into your own home.

Lokanta is the name of a Turkish dining establishment with an informal atmosphere. Guests are able to sit on a patio, eating and talking for as long as they please. This book, named after these pleasant eateries, hopes to accentuate the Turkish enjoyment of food and dining.

Turkey

Lokanta refers to the pleasure of consuming Turkish cuisine. The name comes from the local eating places where the food is cooked with flavour and care. Now that more and more people are visiting Turkey, we are becoming used to a wider variety of Turkish dishes than the already well-known doner and kebabs. And it quite quickly becomes clear that Turkey, in addition to a refined eating culture, also offers healthy meals containing a large variety of fresh fruits and vegetables. Moreover, the ingredients are familiar to those outside the country. This cookbook contains more than 70 mouth-watering recipes accompanied by handy tips and interesting information – for breakfast, lunch, dinner and parties. In this way you can also experience the joy and unique atmosphere of Turkish dining at home.

6

TIME FOR EATING

People in Turkey take the time to eat and even the smallest stall has tables and chairs for its customers. This is because, in addition to taste and smell, atmosphere is just as important in the Mediterranean eating culture.

In the Turkish kitchen, the taste of the ingredients is only the starting point. The varied climate offers a wide variety of fish and meat. The Black Sea offers interesting fish varieties, such as anchovies (hamsi), because the water temperature is relatively low. Furthermore, the country is characterised by a diversity of grains, fruits and vegetables. Every vegetable market is a magnet for those looking for quality ingredients, from average consumers to restaurant owners. The quality of the meals in restaurants and lokantas is very good, which is why many people often eat outside of the home. Turkish meals are generally very healthy as they contain a lot of fresh fruits and vegetables. Vegetables like cucumbers, courgettes and aubergines are often smaller than people in the UK are used to but for that reason, they are much richer in taste.

The aubergine is very popular and is even called the queen of the vegetables. More than two hundred recipes exist for Her Majesty. A lot of vegetables are stuffed with a rice mixture and served lukewarm. All stuffed vegetables (for example, aubergine, tomato, square paprikas, courgettes and white cabbage leaves) are called dolma. But stuffed mussels (midye dolma) – a pure culinary delight – also belong to this category.

To keep vegetables like paprika, pepper, aubergine and okra (bamya) for the winter months, they are hung up on a thread to dry. If you walk through any residential area in Turkey you will see colourful peppers, aubergines and paprikas hanging on clotheslines. Many people also have vine branches and in the spring, the leaves that grow on the branches are blanched and pickled in salt. In these leaves the famous salma is rolled, a rice mixture that absorbs the flavours of the wine leaf. In a lot of residential areas a truck comes in the evening which is fully loaded with water- or honey melons,

TURKISH COFFEE AND TEA

Turkish mocha is a coffee which is very finely ground. To make the coffee you put it unfiltered in a small jug (cezve). For every mocha-cup of water, mix 1 teaspoon of coffee and one lump of sugar and heat slowly. The first foam is carefully scooped into the cups. After this you should stop stirring. From the moment the coffee starts coming up, take it from the hob and pour it into the cups. Never allow Turkish coffee to boil. Do not drink the bottom layer: it is a kind of tradition that after you finish your coffee, you place your cup upside down on the saucer and study the patterns that emerge in the grounds. The future of the coffee drinker is discussed based on the results. Health, career and, of course, love are dealt with in detail.

Turkish tea is mostly made in a demilk (double teapot). The bottom can contain hot water, the top one strong tea extract. Tea is served in tulip-shaped glasses on a saucer with a raised edge. Tea is often drunk quite sweet, with two or three lumps of sugar. The tea, which is put on a charcoal fire after a barbeque, has a light smoky flavour and tastes exceptional.

TURKISH YOGHURT

Turkish cooking is simply not feasible without yoghurt. Yoghurt makes its appearance at the breakfast table and remains there for every major meal of the day. It plays the main role in sauces, in classic dishes such as Iskender kebab and manti (ravioli) and in cacik the widely-eaten yoghurt cucumber salad. The most used Turkish yoghurt is the suzme variant, which is much more solid than normal yoghurt. Farmer's markets also sell yoghurt made from sheep or goat's milk yoghurt Sometimes people prefer to make the yoghurt themselves by leaving fresh cooked farmer's milk to stand with a spoonful of yoghurt. The yoghurt drink ayran is very popular in Turkey and is sold in plastic beakers everywhere. In the UK, Turkish yoghurt is mostly sold in litre-sized containers in Turkish shops.

often weighed out on old Roman scales. A dish of cold melons and ice cubes is often served after a meal. Turks prefer to eat rice with their meals and it's therefore no surprise that the country cultivates 15 types of rice. In areas where rice does not grow very well, people eat bulgur as replacement. Bulgur is cooked, dried and broken wheat that is broken into different sizes. The fine ones are used to make köfte (minced meat dishes) and the larger variant for the pilavs.

Dough is an essential part of the Turkish kitchen. The most famous example is that of the croissant, which has its origins in Asia Minor. Bread is baked fresh several times a day, but simit, ring breads especially in the morning. The börek (puff pastry dishes) are filled with sheep cheese, minced lamb or spinach. Sac ekmek: very thin bread pancakes, which roasted on a charcoal fire, taste just heavenly. Also very good are the filled crepes which are fried on a curved cast iron plate. The dough is rolled very thinly with a long wooden stick. In every market, on every street corner and in all of the parks you can get gözleme with a small glass of strong tea.

FROM BREAKFAST TO EVENING MEAL

A typical Turkish breakfast consists of bread, thick yoghurt, honey or honeycomb, rosebud jam or a rich jam made from quince fruit, fig or subtropical fruits. No breakfast is complete without some slices of tomato with oil, white cheese and black olives. Furthermore a lot of people like to brunch in the weekends with a filled omelette (menemen), fried vegetables (kizartma) and a bowl of soup. Turks always drink black tea in the morning. Although a lot of coffee came into Europe by the way of Turkish armies, the Turks themselves hardly

ever have coffee with their breakfast. That is why the Turkish word for breakfast is kavalti, which literally means 'before the coffee'. At lunchtime Turks often have a first course: soup, fresh salads (shepherd's salad), a meat dish and ayran. The last dish is a refreshing, lightly salted yoghurt drink. On hot summer days Turks will simply eat a light snack at lunchtime, like a grilled corncob, or the wonderful filled mussels (mideye) which you can buy on the street. The evening meal starts with several different warm and cold small snacks (meze), such as stuffed grape leaves, olives and sheep cheese. These are most often served on a big metal tray (tepsi), with small glasses of raki (aniseed liqueur). After that, a meat dish with a pilav (rice or grain dish) and several side dishes are served. Ideally, fresh bread straight out of the oven is served with every course. The dinner gradually comes to an end with some fresh fruit and sweet baklava or rice puddings. After that, a cup Turkish coffee, possibly with a glass of rose liqueur and a piece of Turkish delight (lokum) is served, often followed by a bowl of nuts, sunflower or pumpkin pips. In lokantas

the waiters often come round with a bottle of lemon perfume to freshen up your hands after you have asked for the bill.

Certain dishes are typical for festivities, such as the sugar feast or a wedding. Often these dishes have graceful names like 'women's thighs', 'the lips of a lady' or 'the imam who fainted.' Sometimes festivities are introduced with a duo who create music on a wooden wind instrument and a drum (davul-zurna). You will then see people on the street, young and old dancing and clapping.

ALCOHOL

People in Turkey are not averse to a glass of alcohol. The national drink is aniseed liqueur, raki, which a lot of people call lion's milk (aslant sütü). If you would like to try it, put a bit of raki in a glass and thin it down with water. The drink then becomes cloudy, just like pastis. Serve the lion's milk with ice cubes. In the past raki was often made illegally from figs, raisins or sometimes mulberry. These drinks were very much appreciated by experts. Raki is nowadays often distilled from wine and flavoured with aniseed.

ROOTS

The Turkish kitchen has roots in several culinary traditions. Kebabs, for which you only need a small fire, come from Central-Asia. This was the area where the original Turks herded their sheep, goats and cows. The Mediterranean kitchen also plays a big role and its influence is mainly found in the use of parsley, dill and olive oil. Most influential on the contemporary Turkish kitchen, however, is the court culture that existed during the height of the Ottoman Empire. Cooks used to compete with each other for ingredients and creating new recipes and ingredients but a culinary unity was gradually formed.

With historic cities such as Troy and Constantinople, traces of the Byzantine cultures and the Greek-Roman runes Turkey forms a link between Europe and Asia, both historically and geographically. Lokanta is a cookbook for everyone who wants to be tempted by the full flavours of this wonderful country.

PICKLES

Turks like to eat pickled vegetables (tursu) with their meal. Pickling was originally a way to be keep vegetables for the winter months. But nowadays a raki table (an elaborate evening filling meal consisting of different snacks with which people drink raki) is not complete without tursu. For people who would like to try bibers (a light green paprika that can be sweet or sharp) you can easily pickle them yourself with some bay leaves, vinegar and salt water in an airtight pot.

Yarasin: Enjoy your meal!

12

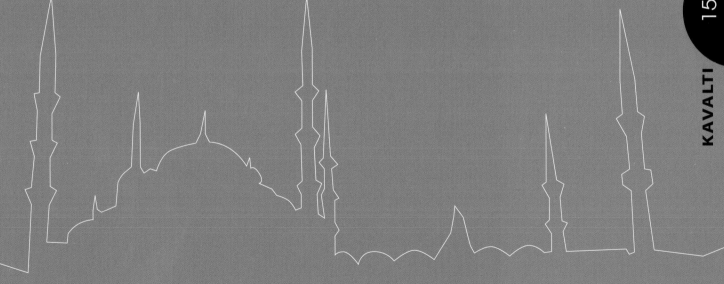

Kavaltı

Simit

Bread Rings

500g (1.10 lbs) wheat flour • 15g (0.52 oz) dried yeast • 200 ml (6.8 fl.oz) lukewarm water • 200 ml lukewarm milk • 2 eggs • 2 tsp salt • 1 tbsp sugar • 250g (8.81oz) butter, melted • 3 tbsp white sesame seed • olive oil

1 Mix the yeast with the lukewarm water and add the milk after 1 minute.
2 Add half of the flour all the while kneading the dough, then 1 egg, the salt, the sugar and the butter.
3 Mix the rest of the flour through the mixture. Knead the dough for 5 minutes.
4 Leave to rest in a bowl that has been greased with butter. Pour some olive oil on it and cover the bowl up with a wet towel. Leave the dough to rise for about 25 minutes.
5 Knead the dough again briefly and divide it into 12 pieces.
6 Roll out each piece and make rings with a diameter of 5-10cm and about 3cm thick. Put these on a baking tray that has been greased with butter.
7 Whisk the rest of the egg loosely and cover the rings with it. Sprinkle them generously with sesame seeds.
8 Leave to rise for another 20 minutes. In the meantime preheat the oven to 180°C (350F, Gas 4).
9 Bake the rolls for 20 minutes until they are golden brown. Serve them warm, with, for example, quince fruit or rosebuds jam.

ON A STICK Those who know Turkey will know that simit (bread rings) is sold on long sticks, usually from carts or on the streets. In addition you see more and more specialized bakeries that offer several varieties of simit, rather like bagel shops.

Ayva receli

Quince fruit jam

1kg (2.2lbs) ripe quince fruits, in thick slices • 400ml (13.5 fl.oz) water • 1kg (2.2lbs) sugar • 1 lemon, squeezed and sieved • baking soda • 4 jam pots

18

TEMPTING AROMA The golden quinces that symbolised love and happiness to the ancient Greeks were brought to England by the Romans. Harvesting time is in October. Many people in Turkey have a tree in their garden. In almost every Turkish shop in the UK you can buy them. The flesh of the quince fruit is harder than that of the normal pear and when cooked and sweetened, its characteristic, tempting aroma is released.

1 Cook the quince fruits for 5-6 minutes gently in the water (less ripe quince fruits need 20-30 minutes).
2 Add the sugar and dissolve through stirring.
3 Boil briefly until the desired thickness has been reached.
4 Add the lemon juice and bring to boil again. Take off the fire and leave to rest for a while.
5 In the meantime put some soda in each pot and pour boiling water on it. Clean out thoroughly with boiling water and fill the pots with the jam. Put the lids on top and turn the pots upside down for a few minutes.
6 Serve with bread and butter.

Soslu biber kızartması

Fried bibers with tomato sauce

200g (7.05fl.oz) whole bibers (light green paprikas) • 2-3 tbsp olive oil • For the sauce: 3 ripe tomatoes, peeled and seeds removed, in pieces • 2 tbsp olive oil • 2 cloves of garlic, crushed • 1 tbsp vinegar • 3 tbsp Turkish yoghurt • salt and cayenne pepper to taste

20

LONG PAPRIKA (sivri biber) is an elongated, white-green paprika that from the outside looks more like a chilli pepper. It is sold at every Turkish shop. Ask for the sweet sort because the peppery sort (often the dark green one) might be too sharp for your dish. In other shops they are sometimes sold under the name 'point paprika'.

1 Wash the bibers and dry them well. Heat the oil and fry the bibers until they become brown and limp. Leave them to drain on kitchen paper.
2 To make the sauce, fry the tomatoes for 10 minutes in hot oil. Sprinkle some salt on top of them.
3 When the tomatoes are soft add the crushed garlic and vinegar and take the pan from the fire.
4 If you like you can sprinkle some cayenne pepper on top and garnish with thick Turkish yoghurt. Serve the fried bibers with the sauce and some bread.

Menemen

Scrambled eggs with vegetables

4 eggs • 2 tbsp butter or olive oil • 2 large onions, chopped • 2-4 bibers (light green sweet or sharp paprikas), seeds removed and in small pieces • 3 beefsteak tomatoes, peeled and in pieces • ½ a bunch of fresh parsley, finely cut • salt and black pepper

22

SAVOURY Savoury snacks are also part of a Turkish breakfast. Often these are bits of sheep or goat feta, a few slices of tomato, black olives and small salted cucumbers.

1 Melt the butter in a large frying pan and fry the onions and bibers on a low flame.
2 Add the tomatoes and after that the parsley, salt and black pepper.
3 Whisk the eggs in a bowl and add them to the mixture. Stir one time and fry for 3-5 minutes. Serve with Turkish bread.

Yayla çorbası

Yoghurt soup

1l (33.8fl.oz) chicken broth (homemade or store bought) • 125g (4.40oz) rice, washed • 500ml (17fl.oz) whole yoghurt • 1 tbsp flour • 1 egg • 2 tbsp butter • 2 tsp dried mint • 2 tsp chilli flakes • pepper and salt

24

SOUP BAR Both soup and yoghurt are essential to the Turkish culinary tradition. Nowadays you can find a soup bar in almost every Turkish city. Many of them start serving their customers at the break of dawn when people are trying to prevent a hangover. Yoghurt soup is so popular that it is also available as a ready-made meal.

1　Bring the broth to the boil. Add the rice to the boiling broth and boil gently for 15 minutes.
2　Remove the pan from the heat and allow to cool for 10 minutes.
3　In the meantime mix the yoghurt, flour and the egg in a bowl. Add this mixture to the soup and put the pan back on the fire.
4　Keep stirring, but take care not to boil the soup. Add salt and pepper to taste.
5　Meanwhile melt the butter and throw in the mint and chilli flakes.
6　Portion the soup into the bowls. Drizzle the butter mixture over the soup.

Sucuklu yumurta

Omelette with spicy sausage

4-6 eggs • 250g (8.81oz) sucuk (dried sausage), grazed and in pieces • 100ml (3.4fl.oz) water • 1 tbsp olive oil • 1-2 large tomatoes, in slices or cubes • 1-2 bibers (light-green sharp or sweet paprika's), fried • 8 black olives

DRIED MEAT The Huns from Central Asia mostly tended sheep, goats and cows. They preserved meat by smearing it with salt and herbs and drying it in the sun. This was called pastirma and it is today sold in slices. People also used to make sausages from lamb and beef flavoured with a lot of garlic. These are called sucuk and in addition to scrambled eggs, they are a well-loved breakfast meal for the weekend.

1   Place the water and pieces of sausage in a pan and boil for 5 minutes with the lid on. Check regularly to see check if the liquid has been absorbed.
2   Melt the butter and fry the sausage for 1-2 minutes.
3   Lower the heat and add the eggs. Stir once gently and cover with the lid.
4   After 5 minutes take the pan off the heat and serve warm. Serve with the tomatoes, bibers and olives.

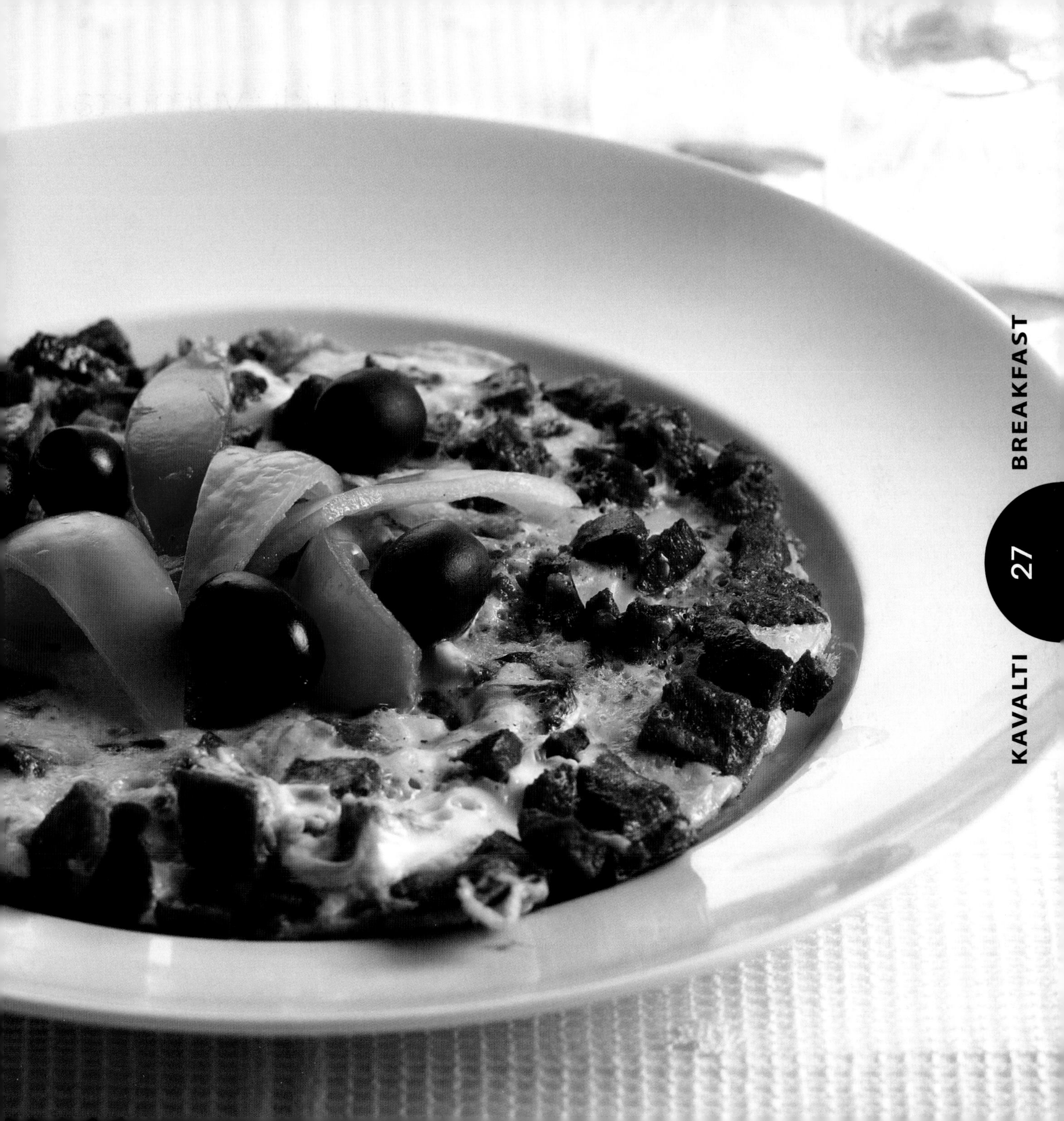

Poğaça

Cheese roll

125g (4.40oz) butter • 200ml (6.8 fl.oz) yoghurt • 4 tbsp olive oil • salt • 2 eggs (1 whole egg, 1 egg yolk only) • 1 tbsp baking powder • 500g (1.10 lbs) flour • 100g (3.52oz) goat or sheep cheese, crumbled.

1 Mix the butter, yoghurt, olive oil, salt and 1 egg. Stir the baking powder through the mixture.
2 Add the flour in bits so the mixture absorbs the flour well.
3 Knead several minutes and leave the dough to rest for 10-20 minutes. Preheat the oven at 180°C, 350F, Gas 4.
4 Divide the dough into pieces the size of a walnut. Press them flat till they become oval forms the size of the palm of your hand.
5 Put 1 tbsp of the cheese on one half of the dough and fold the other half over it. Close the seams well. Repeat this until the dough and cheese are finished.
6 Put the packages on a buttered oven dish and smear them with egg yolk. Bake the rolls for approximately 20 minutes in the oven. Serve with tea.

TIP: Replace the cheese with mashed, cooked potatoes or blanched wild spinach with some cayenne pepper. Alternatively, sprinkle the rolls with cumin seeds.

Antepli helva

Helva with pistachio nuts

200g (7.05oz) sesame paste (tahini) • 100g (3.52oz) honey • 100g (3.52oz) sugar • 100g (3.52oz) unsalted pistachio nuts, pealed • ½ tsp vanilla sugar • 1 tsp lemon juice

1 Thoroughly combine all ingredients with a blender or food processor.
2 Form the mixture into the shape of a rectangular log.
3 Leave the log to chill in the fridge and serve in slices.

Haticenin böreği

Potato onion turban

4 sheets yufka (thin filo dough) • 3-5 tbsp sunflower or olive oil • 100ml (3.4fl.oz) yoghurt of milk • 2 eggs, whisked • For the filling: 3 big onions, finely chopped • 3 tbsp butter • 4 big potatoes, cooked, peeled and mashed • ½ bunch of parsley or mint, finely chopped • 1 tsp chilli flakes • 2 tsp paprika powder • salt

1. To make the filling fry the onions for 3 minutes in butter in a frying pan until they are glazed. Add the potatoes and fry while stirring for another 5 minutes.
2. Add the parsley, chilli flakes, paprika powder and a pinch of salt. Stir and take off the hob.
3. Grease an oven dish with a diameter of 30-35cm (11.8-13.8ins.) with butter. Preheat the oven on 180°C (350F, Gas 4).
4. Put a sheet of yufka on your work space and sprinkle some oil on it. Spread the potato mixture over the sheet.
5. Make a roll of the sheet until it looks like a long string. Moisten with some yoghurt, oil and egg.
6. Take one end and turn the rest of the string over it like a spiral. Repeat with the other sheets and in this way making 4 rolls. Spread the rest of the yoghurt, oil and egg on top of the rolls.
7. Bake for 15 minutes golden brown in the oven. Serve warm with tea, as a snack or as a first course.

BREAD This typical bread is also known as kömbe. The mode of preparation comes from the villages of Camşik (Sivas, Divriği).

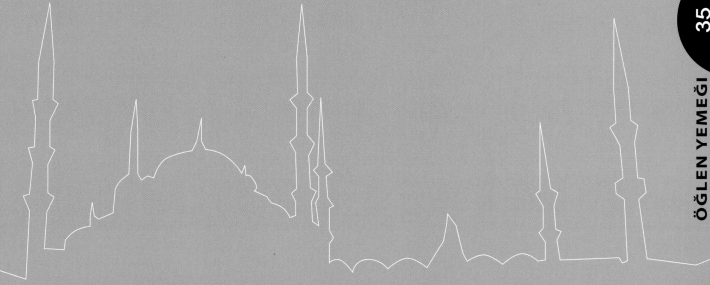

Öğlen yemeği

Ayran

Refreshing yoghurt drink

½ glass thick organic yoghurt • ½ glass of water • salt to taste • ice cubes (optional)

36

THIRST QUENCHER
Aside from tea, ayran is the most consumed drink in Turkey. People begin drinking it from lunchtime onwards. The yoghurt drink is a good thirst quencher, particularly with high temperatures in summer. The idea is a very old one: in the past, the nomads diluted the sieved yoghurt with water from the wells they came across on their journeys. Currently it is much easier as you can simply buy ayran in plastic cups.

1   Whisk the yoghurt and the salt with a whisk through the water (or mix in a blender).
2   Serve cold. Ice cubes can be added if preferred.

Mercimek çorbası

Red lentil soup

150g (5.29oz) red lentils, washed • 1l (33.8fl.oz) chicken broth (homemade or store bought) • 1 tbsp flour • 2 tbsp butter • 1 onion, finely chopped • 1 tbsp concentrated tomato puree • 1 small carrot, in pieces • 2 cloves of garlic, finely cut • 2 tsp dried mint • 1 tsp chilli flakes • 1 lemon, in slices • salt

TIP: Although this soup is normally made with red lentils, you can also use yellow lentils. Soup often tastes better the following day as the flavours have had time to blend. The only thing you may have to do is add some water to thin the soup down.

1 Melt 1 tbsp of butter and stir the flour through for 2 minutes until it turns light brown.
2 Add the lentils, onion, tomato puree and carrot. Fry while stirring for a few minutes.
3 Add broth, garlic and salt and bring to boil while stirring constantly. Leave to cook for 20-30 minutes until the vegetables are done, then blend with a mixer.
4 Melt the rest of the butter and add mint and chilli flakes. Leave for a short while bubbling on a high flame. Pour in the soup and stir briefly. Serve warm with lemon slices to taste.

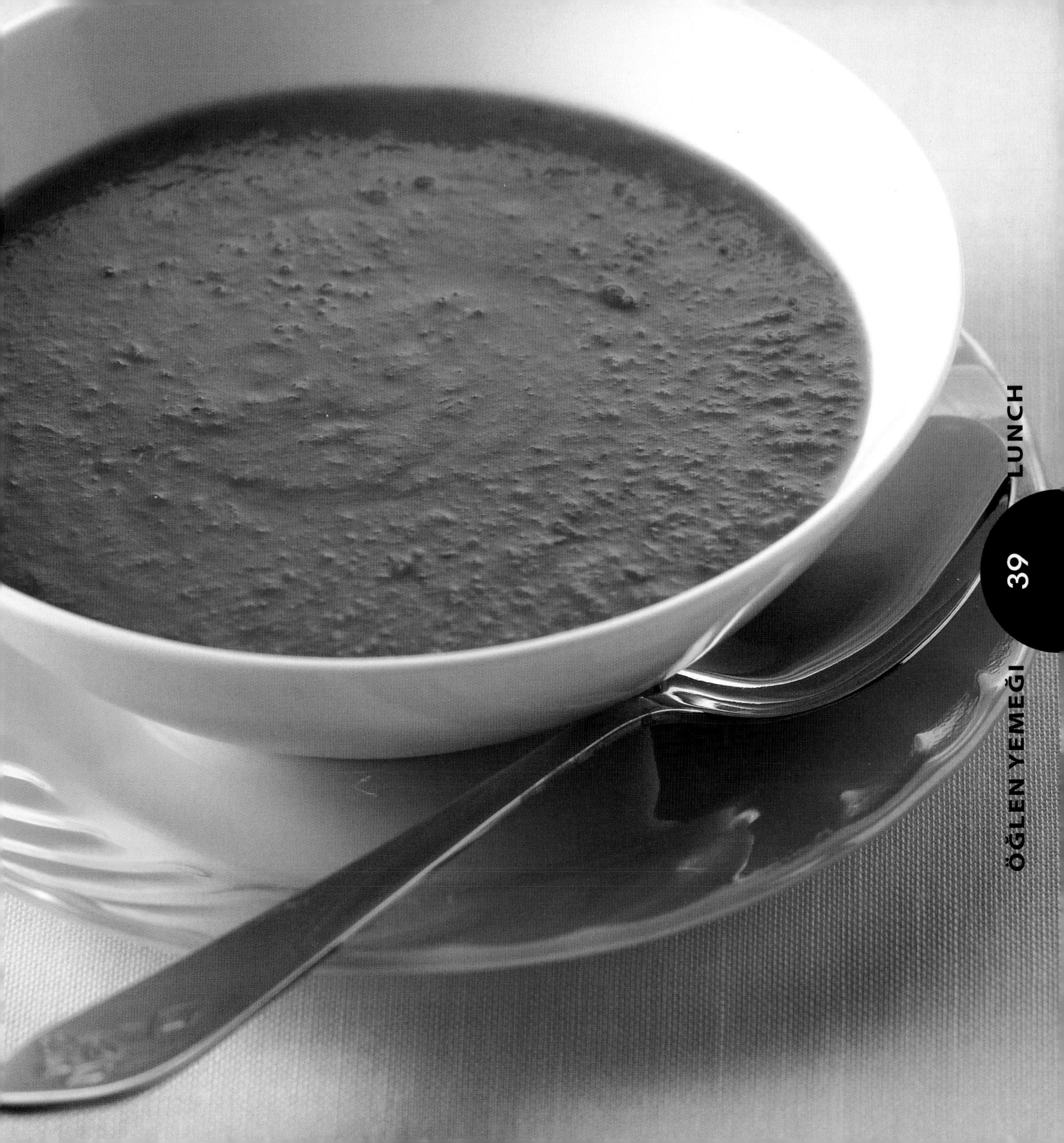

Lahmacun

Turkish pizza

500g (1.10 lbs) flour • 10g (0.35oz) dried yeast • 1 tsp salt • 1 tsp sugar • 400ml (13.5fl.oz) lukewarm water • 1 red onion, in thin rings • 2 tbsp fresh parsley, finely cut • 1 tbsp lemon juice • For the filling: 200g (7.05oz) minced lamb • 1 white onion, cut into small pieces • 1 tomato, peeled and cut into small pieces • 1 tsp paprika puree (see box) • 1 tsp tomato puree • 1 tsp salt • 1 tsp black pepper • 1 tsp chilli flakes

A POT OF PUREE Puree of red paprika is sold in glass pots in Turkish shops. In Turkish it is called tatli biber salcasi. Only use small amounts because the puree is very concentrated. Paprika puree is used more often than paprika powder, although the powder can be used as a replacement for the puree. A variant of this dish, which is called acili biber salcasi is a little sharper in taste as a result of the pepper added. A lot of people make this puree themselves and throughout the residential areas you can see the little peppers hanging on washing lines, drying in the warm Turkish sun.

1 Mix the flour with the yeast, the salt and the sugar. Make a hole and pour 300ml water in it. Mix the water with the flour.
2 Knead the mixture well and add the same amount of water so that a nice smooth dough is the result. Leave this to rest for 45 minutes under a wet towel in a warm place.
3 In the meantime mix the ingredients for the filling in the mixer until it becomes a smooth puree. If the puree is too dry you can add some milk.
4 Preheat the oven to 220°C. Divide the dough in portions the size of a kiwi fruit. Spread them out relatively thin in the form of a circle with a diameter of 20cm on workspace that is covered in flour.
5 Grease an oven tray with oil. Divide the filling in a thin layer over the pizzas.
6 Bake them for 10 minutes or until the filling is thoroughly cooked. The bottom should not become hard.
7 Sprinkle the pizzas with the onion rings, parsley and the lemon juice. Serve rolled up in a serviette or wrapped in aluminium foil (covered halfway).

Çoban salatası

Shepherd's salad

1 red onion, in halved rings • salt • 2 big tomatoes, in pieces • 2 long bibers (sweet or sharp Turkish paprika), pips removed and in pieces • 1 small cucumber, in pieces • 4 tbsp fresh parsley, finely cut • 8 black olives, for garnishing • For the dressing: 4 tbsp lemon juice • 5 tbsp olive oil • 1 tsp vinegar • 1 tsp salt • 1 tsp black pepper

1 Rub the onion rings with salt. Rinse off the salt with water after 5 minutes.
2 Mix all ingredients for the salad except the olives and put them on a dish.
3 Mix the ingredients for the dressing and pour these over the salad. Leave to rest for half an hour so that the flavours can interact with each other. Garnish with olives.

Fasulye piyazı

White bean salad

200g (7.05oz) dried white beans • 1 tomato, finely cut • 1 spring onion, cut in thin slices • 3 tbsp fresh parsley, finely cut • 8 black olives, for garnishing • 1 finely cut tomato or tursu (pickled vegetable), or grated carrot, for garnishing • For the dressing: 2 tbsp lemon juice • 2 tbsp olive oil • 1 tsp vinegar 1 tsp salt • 1 tsp black pepper

44

PICKLES Just like in the Indian kitchen, people in Turkey generally like to eat some pickled vegetables with their meal. Pickling was originally a way to preserve vegetables for the winter months. But nowadays, for most people a raki table (a meal that consists completely of meze) is only complete if tursu is served with it. Often it consists of (often sharp) bibers that are pickled in white wine vinegar with some sea salt, pepper corns and sugar.

1 Leave the beans overnight to soak in water. If you canned beans, you can skip this step.
2 Cook the beans for 30 minutes until well done. Rinse them with cold water.
3 Mix all ingredients for the salad except the garnish and put them on a dish.
4 Mix the ingredients for the dressing and pour them over the salad. Garnish with the tomato, tursu or carrot.

Patlıcan ezmesi

Aubergine-yoghurt salad

1kg (2.2lbs) aubergines, halved • 500ml (17fl.oz) yoghurt • 100ml (3.4fl.oz) olive oil • 1 tsp lemon juice • 3-4 bibers (sweet or hot, depending on your preference), seeds removed • 4-5 cloves of garlic • 3 Turkish green dolma paprikas (see further) • 2 tomatoes, in pieces • 2 tbsp fresh parsley, finely cut • salt

46

RICH IN TASTE Dolma paprikas (dolmalik biber) are as big as an egg and rather angular. Because they are so small, the taste is very rich. They are usually stuffed with a rice mixture, which is why they are called dolma.

TIP: For a really delicious flavour, try grilling the aubergines on a barbeque instead of the frying pan.

1   Leave the aubergines for 30 minutes in salt water. Rinse them and fry the aubergines on a high flame in some olive oil.
2   Pull the blackened peel off the aubergines. Mash the pulp with the rest of the olive oil and the lemon juice.
3   Pound the bibers with the garlic in a mortar until it becomes a paste or use a food processor. Mix the aubergine mash and the yoghurt.
4   Grill the paprikas for 10 minutes and remove the blackened skin.
5   Serve the aubergine mash with the paprika and tomato. Garnish with parsley.

Mantı

Dough cushions with three different sauces

For the dough: 500g (1.10lbs) flour • ½ tsp salt • 2 eggs • 75ml (2.5fl.oz) lukewarm water • For the filling: 250g (8.81oz) minced meat • 2 small onions, finely cut • 3 tbsp fresh parsley, finely cut • pepper and salt • For the sauces: olive oil • 1 tomato, in small pieces • ½ of a red pepper, seeds removed, finely cut • 250ml (8.5fl.oz) yoghurt • 2-4 cloves of garlic, pounded in a mortar until it becomes a paste • 100g (3.52oz) butter • 1 tsp chilli flakes • 1 tbsp dried mint

1 Sieve the flour in a big bowl. Add the salt. Make a little hole and break the eggs into it.
2 Stir the eggs through the flour. In the meantime gradually add the water.
3 Knead for about 8 minutes until it becomes a smooth dough. Divide the dough in 3 portions, make into balls and cover them for 10 minutes with a moist towel.
4 To make the filling, mix the minced meat, onion and the parsley. Add salt and pepper to taste. Stir well and put aside for a while.
5 Roll out the first dough ball so that it becomes a patch that is 1-2mm thick on a working space which is sprinkled with flour. Now cut the patch into squares of about 3-4cm.
6 Scoop 1 tsp minced meat in the middle of the square. Bring the points together and firmly press the edges. Repeat with the rest of the dough.
7 Bring 2 litre salted water to boil in a big pan. Add the cushions and stir softly. Leave for 4 minutes without lid to simmer on a low flame. Stir occasionally without damaging the pasta.
8 To make the tomato sauce braise the tomato for 5 minutes in a pan with a bit of oil. Add the fresh red pepper and keep warm.
9 To make the yoghurt sauce, mix the yoghurt with the garlic paste.
10 To make the butter sauce, melt the butter with the chilli flakes and dried mint.
11 Take the pasta cushions (manti) out of the water (keep the water to make broth). First scoop some yoghurt sauce over the manti and then the tomato sauce. Sprinkle with some butter sauce.

48

TIP: This mini ravioli is also called kayseri mantisi. Mince meat, minced chicken fillet or feta can be used as a filling. In Bolu, the winter sports area of Turkey, manti is served with walnuts and cheese. If you are in a hurry you can buy the manti in dried form, as it can be quite time consuming to make it from scratch.

Beyaz balık ve soğan piyazı

Fried fish fillet with onion salad

500g (1.10 lbs) filet of white fish • 1 tsp sea salt • 1 tsp black pepper • 2 twigs of dill, finely chopped • 10 bay leaves • 2 lemons, in thin slices • olive oil • For the salad: 500g (1.10 lbs) onions, in thin halves of rings • 1 tbsp see salt • 3 tbsp olive oil • 1 tbsp lemon juice • 50g (1.76oz) black olives without seeds • 3 tbsp fresh parsley, finely chopped • pepper and salt

50

1 Preheat the oven on 180°C (350F, Gas 4). Sprinkle the filets with salt and pepper and leave for 5 minutes.
2 Put them together with the dill and bay leaves in an oven dish that is greased with oil. Cover with the lemon slices.
3 Bake the fish until it is cooked for 20 minutes in the oven. Remove the bay leaves before serving.
4 In the meantime, make the onion salad. Sprinkle the onion rings with salt and leave for 5 minutes.
5 Rinse the onion rings and press out the liquid.
6 Mix the onion with oil, lemon juice, olives, parsley, pepper and salt. Serve with the fish.

Midye dolması

Stuffed mussels

1kg (2.2lbs) big mussels • 300ml (10.2fl.oz) water • a dash of white wine (of your own choice) • 2 lemons, in slices • For the filling: 500g (1.10 lbs) onions, finely cut • 200g (7.05oz) long grained rice, washed • 100g (3.52oz) pine nuts, coarsely chopped • 100g (3.52oz) sultanas, steeped • 150ml (5.1fl.oz) hot water, for the rice • 1 tbsp sugar • 1 tbsp thyme • 1 tsp cinnamon • 8 twigs of parsley, finely chopped • 8 twigs of dill, finely chopped • olive oil • salt

1 Scrub if necessary the mussels clean under streaming water. Throw away the damaged mussels and the ones that do not close when tapped.
2 Carefully open the rest with a knife and cut the flesh and the beard out. Check for mud or stones. Wash well and leave to drain. Save the shells.
3 Glaze the onions for 2-3 minutes in olive oil. Add the rice, pine nuts and sultanas. Cook while stirring for 5 minutes.
4 Add the hot water, a pinch of salt and the sugar. Leave on a low flame for 5-10 minutes to simmer until all the liquid has been absorbed.
5 Add the thyme, cinnamon, parsley and dill and cover the pan with a lid. Take from the fire and leave to cool for 10 minutes.
6 Fill the mussel meat with as much rice mixture that fits. Push the mussel edges closed again and put the mussel back in its shell.
7 Put the filled mussels in a big pan and add 300ml water. Leave to simmer while covered on a mild flame for 30-45 minutes. Check if all the liquid has been absorbed.
8 Possibly extinguish with some white wine and leave on the fire for another 5 minutes. After that leave to cool for 10 minutes.
9 Possibly grease the shells in with some oil to make them shiny.
10 Serve with the slices of lemon. Sprinkle the opened mussels with lemon juice and enjoy.

52

LOVED SNACK Midye is sold along the long Turkish coast on the street and at the beach until late in the evening. It is a favoured snack particularly after sunset when it is busy along the boulevards. Midye comes with a shell to use as a spoon.

Döner ekmek

Döner sandwich

300g (10.58oz) tender beef steak, in very thin slices • 150g (5.29oz) lean lamb mince • 1 tbsp butter • 1-2 pide (flat breads), in small square pieces • 150g (5.29oz) butter, melted • 2 tomatoes, grilled • 2 bibers (sweet green paprikas), grilled • pepper and salt

54

TAKE-AWAY Döner is one of the most famous Turkish snacks, which people often eat while on the move. Street stalls cook a large roll of the meat on a rotating spit in front of a gas grill. Vendors cut off slices of meat with a long knife.

1 Pile the slices of steak (alternatively lamb or chicken fillet) in turns with the mince on top of each other. Cover in aluminium foil and put in the freezer for at least 8 hours.
2 Cut the frozen meat in slices and fry for about 1 minute in hot butter with pepper and salt. The meat should stay tender.
3 Heat the bread in the oven. Divide the meat over the bread and sprinkle with the melted butter.
4 Garnish with grilled tomatoes and bibers. Serve with cacik (yoghurt cucumber sauce, see recipe on page 76).

Pide ekmek

Turkish bread

375ml (12.7fl.oz) lukewarm water • 2 tbsp dried yeast • 1 tsp sugar • ½ tsp sea salt • 500g (1.10 lbs) white flour • 4 tbsp olive oil

56

CRUNCHY FRESH Just like in France or Italy, a meal in Turkey is not the same without bread. You always eat pide fresh, because bakeries bake new bread several times a day. When it just comes from the oven it tastes like a big croissant. The variety known lavac is especially recommended.

1   Mix the water, yeast, sugar and salt. Leave standing until bubbles appear.
2   Add half of the flour and all of the olive oil. Knead or whisk the dough until it is elastic and slowly add more flour.
3   When the dough cannot absorb anymore flour, knead it for another 5 minutes.
4   Spread the olive oil over the dough and leave it to rise for an hour in a bowl that has been greased in and covered with a tea towel.
5   Preheat the oven on 220°C (425F, Gas 7). Knead the dough well and divide into three portions. Roll the portions into oval slices.
6   Press holes in the dough with your finger tips and leave for another 15 minutes to rise.
7   Put in the oven and leave the dough to warm up for 2 to 3 minutes. Take out of the oven and stretch the patches until they are 30cm wide so that the bread will become light and fluffy.
8   Put the bread again in the oven and bake it for about 10 minutes.

Yeşil zeytinli börek

Green olive rolls

500g (1.10 lbs) flour • 10g (0.35oz) dried yeast • 2 tsp salt • 1 tsp sugar • 2 tbsp lukewarm water • 350ml (11.9fl.oz) Turkish yoghurt • 4 tbsp olive oil • For the filling: 2 onions, shredded • 2 tbsp olive oil • 500g (1.10 lbs) green olives, finely chopped • 2 tbsp tomato puree • 3 tbsp walnuts, finely chopped • 5 tbsp parsley, finely chopped • pepper and salt

1 Mix the flour with the yeast, the salt and the sugar. Add the lukewarm water drop by drop.
2 Pour the yoghurt and olive oil and knead for 5 minutes until the dough is smooth. Leave to rise for 60 minutes under a towel.
3 Glaze for the filling the onions for 2 minutes in oil and add the olives and tomato puree, nuts, parsley, pepper and salt.
4 Divide the dough into 10 portions and make circles that are 3mm thick.
5 Divide the filling over the dough patches and fold the edges of the dough to the inside.
6 Leave to rest for 15 minutes. Preheat the oven at 180°C (350F, Gas 4). Bake the rolls for 30 minutes. Leave them for 10 minutes to cool under a moist towel before serving.

Peynirli gözleme

Filled crepes with white cheese

250g (8.81oz)   yufka (filo dough) • unsalted butter • For the filling: 100g (3.52oz) white cheese or feta • 100g (3.52oz) tulum (fresh cheese) or ricotta • 1 tsp salt • 1 tsp black pepper

60

WELL-FILLED Gözleme is a loved snack. In Turkey it is prepared on bolted big iron plates above a fire or on gas. Turks in the UK sometimes use cast iron woks that they put upside down on the gas. You can fill gözleme with cheese, potato, parsley, wild spinach, a sort of endive (pazi) or with aubergine and onion. Yufka dough is for sale in packages of A-4 size in which a few large sheets are folded up. You can only keep them for a short time before they become spoiled.

1 Mix the cheeses and bring to taste with salt and pepper.
2 Heat a heavy cast iron pan and melt some unsalted butter.
3 Put a sheet of yufka dough in the pan. Place some filling on and fold it as if you were closing an envelope.
4 Heat for a few minutes until the cheeses melt and then turn over. The dough has to remain soft. Repeat until dough and filling are finished.
5 Serve hot, with a glass of ayran (see recipe on page 36).

Zetinyağlı enginar

Artichokes in olive oil

4 fresh artichoke ends • juice of 1 lemon • 1 potato, peeled and in cubes • 1 carrot, in cubes • 100g (3.52oz) shallots, finely chopped • 1 tsp sugar • salt to taste • 4-6 twigs of dill, stems and leaves separated • 100ml (3.4fl.oz) water

1   Smear the artichoke ends with a bit of lemon juice and rinse them. Place them in a big frying pan.
2   Put the potato, carrot and shallots on the artichokes. Sprinkle with sugar and salt.
3   Add the stems of dill, the rest of the lemon juice and the water and cover the pan with a lid.
4   Bring to boil and leave to simmer on a low flame for about 30 minutes. Check if the vegetables are well cooked.
5   Take off the hob and leave to cool. Serve with the dill leaves (either whole or finely chopped).

İskender kebap

Lamb on bread with tomato-yoghurt sauce

500g (1.10 lbs) lamb, in thin slices • olive oil • 1 large flat bread (pide), in small cubes • For the marinade: 3 tbsp olive oil • juice of 1 lemon • 1 tsp sea salt • 1 tsp black pepper • 2 twigs of thyme • For the tomato sauce: 2 onions, shredded • 2 tbsp olive oil • 2 cloves of garlic, in thin slices • 1 can of tomato cubes • 1 tsp salt • pepper to taste • 3 tbsp fresh parsley, finely chopped • For the yoghurt sauce: 250 ml Turkish yoghurt (süzme) • 3 cloves of garlic, pounded into a paste in a mortar • For the butter sauce: 5 tbsp creamy butter • ½ tsp paprika puree or powder • ½ tsp cayenne pepper

1 Mix the ingredients for the marinade. Leave the meat to marinate for at least a few hours, preferably for 8 hours.
2 Glaze for the tomato sauce the onions and garlic in olive oil. Then add the tomato cubes with the salt and pepper. Leave to simmer for 20 minutes on a low flame.
3 In the meantime stir the garlic paste through the yoghurt.
4 Heat some olive oil and scorch the slices of lamb so they remain pink on the inside.
5 For the butter sauce melt the butter with the paprika puree and cayenne pepper.
6 Divide the bread into pieces and scatter over a dish. Sprinkle half of the butter sauce over the bread.
7 Put the meat on it and first pour the tomato sauce and after that the yoghurt sauce over it. Garnish with what is left over of the butter sauce.

Kısır

Tabaulésalade

125g (4.40oz) tabaulé or couscous • 1 tbsp paprika puree • 3 spring onions, finely cut • 1 cucumber, in pieces • 2 fleshy tomatoes, peeled and cut into small pieces • 8 tbsp fresh parsley, finely cut • 2 tsp chilli flakes (to taste) • 2 tbsp lemon juice or pomegranate syrup (nar suyu) • salt • olive oil • a few olives • lettuce or chicory leaves.

66

REFRESHING Kisir is a refreshing salad based on wheat (tabaulé is broken and steamed wheat with a pleasant nutty taste). It is very nutritious and keeps well. The kisir achieves a very specific taste when you replace the lemon juice with pomegranate syrup. In some areas kisir is also made without cucumber.

1   Make the salad a few hours before serving, so that the tabaulé can absorb the aromas.
2   Put the tabaulé in a dish and pour some boiling water over it so that the tabaulé is just under water. Mix the paprika puree through the tabaulé and leave to soak for 20 minutes.
3   When the tabaulé is absorbed by the water mix it with the spring onion, cucumber, tomato and parsley.
4   Add chilli flakes, lemon juice and salt to taste. Add in drops a bit of olive oil. Serve with olives, salad or chicory leaves and a glass of ayran (see recipe on page 36).

Karnabahar salatası

Cauliflower-coriander salad

1 cauliflower, in small florets • 5 tbsp olive oil • juice of 2 lemons • 1 tbsp paprika puree • 1 tsp salt • ½ tsp black pepper • 3 tbsp coriander, finely chopped

68

1 Boil the cauliflower florets for 10 minutes or until done. Rinse them with cold water.
2 Make a dressing of olive oil, lemon juice, paprika puree, salt and pepper.
3 Pour the dressing over the cauliflower florets and leave to soak for 1 hour. Just before serving sprinkle the salad with the coriander leaves.

Fırında sütlaç

Rice pudding

1l milk • 10 tbsp sugar • 400g (14oz) risotto or pudding rice, washed • 1 tbsp rice flour or corn flour, diluted with water • ½ a packet of vanilla sugar • 1 egg yolk • 1 tsp cinnamon • unsalted pistachio nuts, for garnishing

SWEET CHICKEN In every Turkish shopping street you can find pastry shops specialising in sweets. Lined up underneath the long glass counter are several desserts. Sütlaç is the most famous of these but there are also classics that are made with sugared chicken (tavuk gögsü) or sweetened spinach.

1 Warm the milk with the sugar and rice. Leave 25 minutes to boil on a medium flame.
2 Add the diluted rice, flour and vanilla sugar. Remove from the hob and leave for ten minutes covered with a lid.
3 Preheat the oven for 180°C (350F, Gas 4). Scoop 1 spoonful of milk with rice out of the pan and mix it with the egg yolk and the cinnamon.
4 Portion the rest of the rice from the pan into 4 oven dishes. Brush the egg yolk mixture in equal amounts over the puddings.
5 Bake the puddings in about 5 minutes golden brown. Serve them chilled with unsalted, chopped pistachio nuts.

Kazandıbı

Pudding roll

750ml (25.4fl.oz) milk • 100g (3.52oz) rice flour • 1 tbsp corn flour • 1 tbsp sugar • 1 tbsp butter • 100g (3.52oz) powdered sugar

1 Preheat the oven on 180°C (350F, Gas 4). Heat the milk, rice flour, corn flour and sugar stirring constantly until the mixture thickens.
2 Add the butter and remove the pan from the hob.
3 Sprinkle the powdered sugar evenly over the bottom of a glass oven dish. Pour the milk mixture over it and smooth out the top layer.
4 Put the dish in the oven for about 20 minutes.
5 Take out of the oven and plunge the bottom of the dish in cold water so it cools off quickly, then place the dish in the fridge.
6 Cut the pudding into 4-6 pieces. Roll up each piece carefully with a wooden spoon. Sprinkle with cinnamon powder.

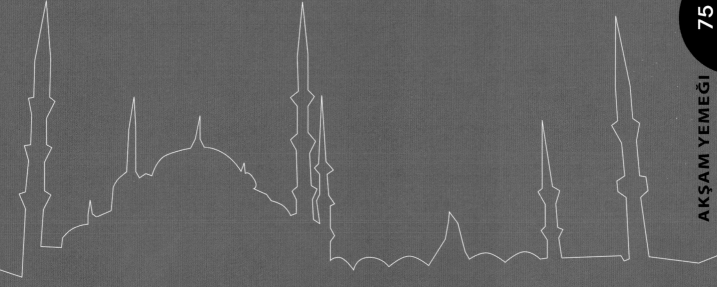

Akşam yemeği

Cacik

Fresh yoghurt cucumber sauce with dill

1 large cucumber, finely grated • 4 twigs dill, finely cut • 2-3 cloves of garlic, pounded in mortar • 250ml (8.5fl.oz) Turkish yoghurt • 2 tbsp olive oil • 1 tsp black pepper • 1 tsp salt • 1 tbsp mint, finely cut (for garnishing)

76

CLASSIC Cacik (pronounced dzjaadzjoek) is a tasty classic from the Turkish kitchen where the dish is considered as a salad. Cacik is served with pilav (rice), bulgur (wheat) and several grilled dishes and kebabs. There are regional differences in the tastes to add such as mint, dill or fresh lemon juice.

1 Put the cucumber in a sieve and press the liquid out.
2 Stir the dill and garlic through the yoghurt.
3 Add the cucumber, olive oil, pepper and salt and stir well.
4 Leave to stand for a few hours and serve cool, garnished with mint. Give everyone their own bowl, placed next to their plate.

Lahana dolması

Stuffed cabbage leaves with rice-onion mixture

---

1 medium white cabbage • For the stuffing: 150ml (5.1fl.oz) olive oil • 2 onions, shredded • 200g (7.05oz) long-grained rice, washed and soaked for 30 minutes • ½ tsp paprika puree or powder • 1 tbsp pine nuts • 1 tbsp sultanas, steeped • 1 tsp salt • 1 tsp black pepper • 3 tbsp fresh parsley, finely chopped • juice of 1 lemon

78

1 Cook the cabbage with some salt for 10 minutes in water. Leave to cool and carefully take away the leaves. Select the leaves which are as big as a hand, but also keep the rest.
2 Remove the hard veins. Cover the bottom of a pan with small or torn cabbage leaves.
3 For the stuffing, heat the olive oil and glaze the onions. Add the rice, paprika puree, pine nuts and sultanas. Bring to taste with salt and pepper.
4 Stir for 2 minutes until the rice is glassy, then add 250ml of water. Leave to simmer for fifteen minutes until the water is absorbed.
5 Add the parsley and the largest part of the lemon juice.
6 Put a cabbage leaf with the veins on top in front of you. On that scoop 1 tsp filling, fold the sides over it and roll up the dolma.
7 Put the dolmas with the veins at the bottom in a broad pan. Add as much water so that all dolmas are under water.
8 Put the leftover cabbage leaves on the dolmas. Cover with a turned down plate and bring to boil.
9 Leave to simmer for 30-45 minutes. Make sure that the pan does not cook dry. Leave the dolmas to cool in the pan with the liquid.

BRIMFUL Dolma means 'stuffed'. Turks enjoy many kinds of stuffed vegetables like aubergine, tomato, courgette and several paprika varieties, but they also like stuffed wine and cabbage leaves and even stuffed mussels. Stuffed wine leaves are called sarma (in full: yaprak sarmasi).

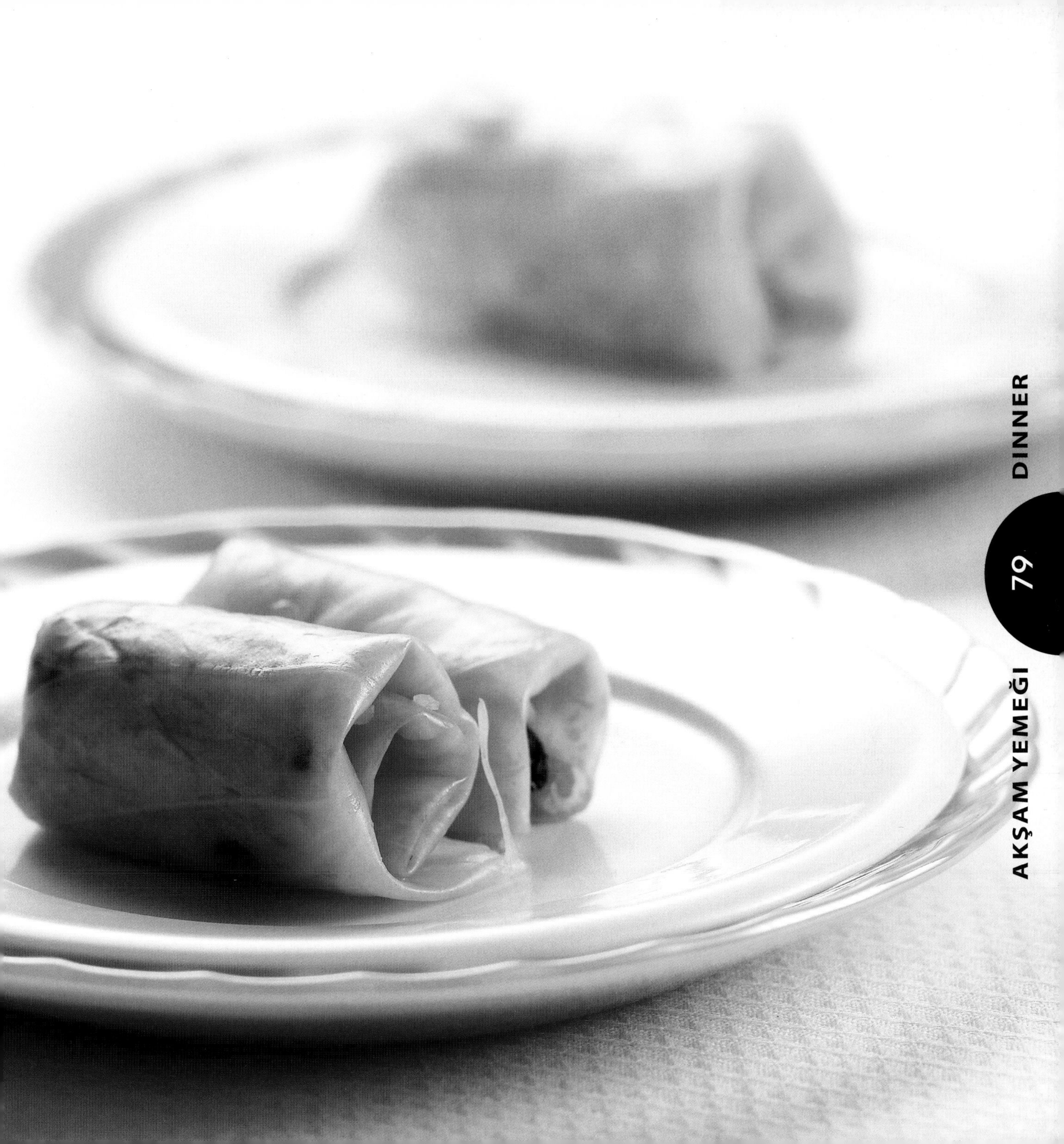

Denizbörülcesi

Glasswort in garlic-olive oil sauce

250g (8.81oz) glasswort • 100ml (3.4fl.oz) olive oil • 2 tomatoes, peeled and in small cubes • 6 cloves of garlic, peeled and halved • 3 tbsp white wine vinegar • juice of 1 lemon • salt

1   Wash the glasswort and blanche it for 3 minutes in boiling water. Leave to drain.
2   Heat the oil and fry the tomatoes and garlic stirring constantly.
3   Add the glasswort and fry it for 2 minutes together with the tomatoes and garlic.
4   Take the vegetables out of the pan and mix with the vinegar and the lemon juice. Taste a piece to see if any salt should be added (take care because glasswort is already quite salty).
5   Serve cooled. Can also be served as meze.

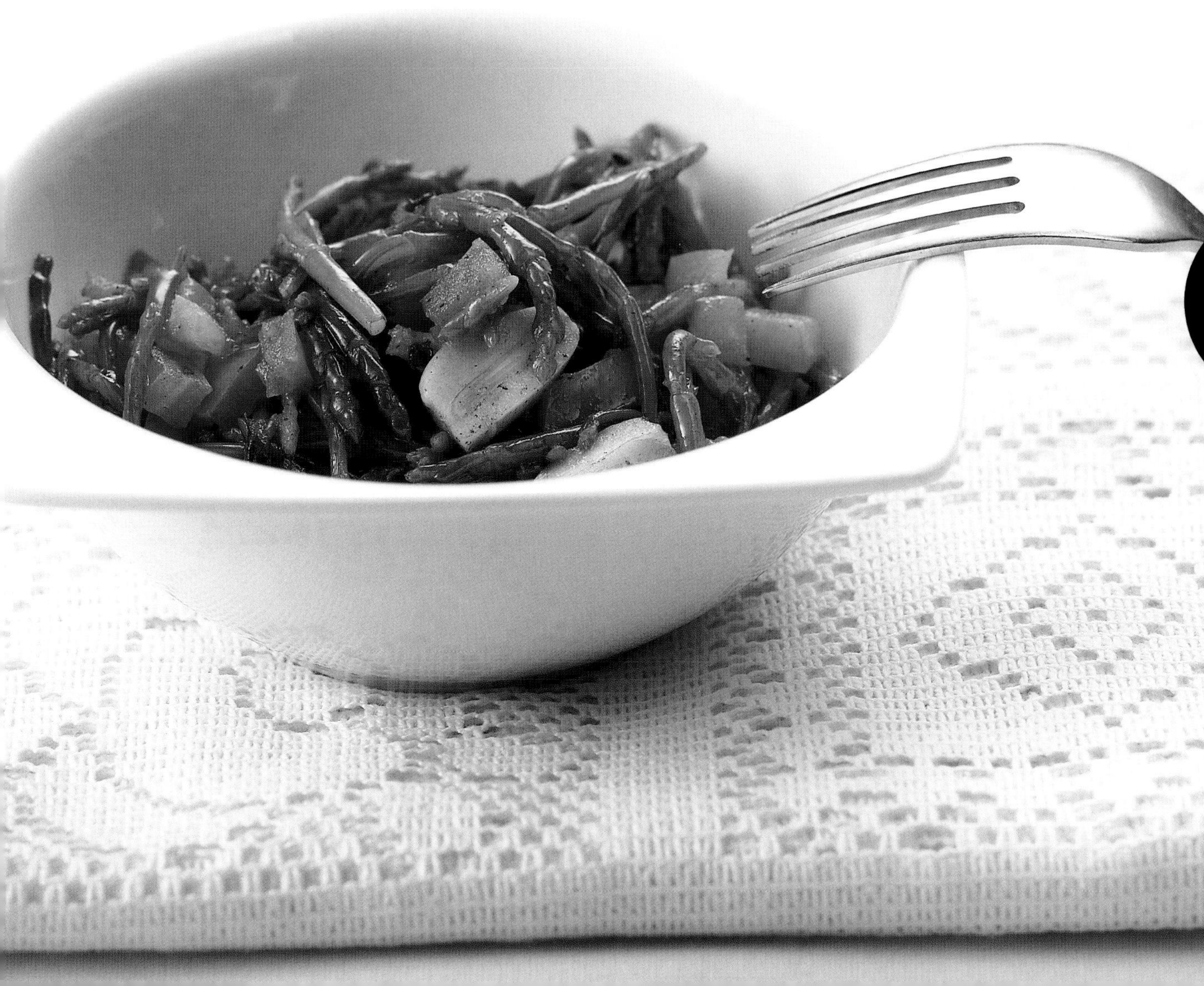

Humus

Chickpea puree

200g (7.05oz) chickpeas, soaked, cooked and with skin removed (or 400g (14oz) chickpeas from a can) • 4 tbsp tahini (sesame paste) • 2-3 cloves of garlic, squeezed • 2 tbsp lemon juice • 2 tbsp olive oil • 1 tsp salt • 1 tsp black pepper • 2 tbsp fresh parsley, finely chopped • black olives

NICE AND SMOOTH
Tahini is a paste made from sesame seeds that you can buy in any Mediterranean or organic shop. The paste keeps for a long time if you store it in a cool place.

1   Mix all the ingredients except the olives in a blender or food processor until it becomes a soft paste. Bring to taste with pepper and salt.
2   Serve cooled on a flat plate with sac (see recipe on page 140) or pide. Garnish with olives and a small amount of olive oil.

Domatesli patlıcan salatası

Tomato-aubergine salad

1 aubergine • 2 tbsp olive oil • 2 ripe tomatoes, peeled and in cubes • 1 white onion, shredded • 2 cloves of garlic in thin slices • 1 tsp sea salt • 1 tbsp parsley for garnishing

84

TIP: Aubergines tend to soak up a lot of oil when they are fried. If you want to prevent that, cook them in the oven or directly over a fire. Always first prick some holes in the unpeeled fruit with a fork and leave it for 1 hour in an oven on the highest temperature setting. This way, the taste of the aubergine is fully reached. Alternatively, aubergine puree is available ready-made in almost every Turkish shop, just like hummus.

1 Peel strips of skin from the aubergines so the outside achieves a striped appearance. Cut the aubergines in two and leave them to soak for 30 minutes in salt water. Rinse them well and dab dry. Cut into cubes.
2 Fry the aubergine in oil, covered with a lid and on a high heat until they are done.
3 Add the tomato cubes with the onion, garlic and sea salt. Leave to simmer for 10 minutes.
4 Mash with a fork until it becomes puree and serve cool. Garnish with some parsley and olive oil.

Tavuklu kadayıf

Crispy chicken with Chinese noodles

1 big chicken fillet • 4-5 broccoli florets, finely cut • 1 small carrot, finely cut • 1 small courgette, finely cut • 4 dough nests (kadayif), broken into little pieces • 75g (2.64oz) white cheese (or feta), crumbled • sunflower oil to deep-fry in • 2 twigs of thyme • For the puree: 4 large potatoes, peeled and in pieces • 200ml (6.8 fl.oz milk • 1 tbsp butter • 1 tsp nutmeg, grated • salt

MIE Kadayif is a relatively thin, dried pasta that looks like Chinese noodles. It is ready-made for use in Turkish shops. Kadayif is also used as the base for a type of baklava dessert; the only thing you have to do when you get home is pour some sugar water over it.

1 Pound the chicken fillet with a meat hammer or bread knife until it is very thin and flat.
2 Cook the broccoli, carrot and courgette in salt water for 5 minutes until well done.
3 For the puree, cook the potatoes until they are done. Mash them with the milk and butter. Add nutmeg and salt to taste.
4 Spread the crumbled dough nests out over your work space. First put the meat on, then the vegetables and then the cheese. Roll up the whole thing in its length.
5 Heat the oil in a broad frying pan and fry the meat for about 10 minutes on both sides. Leave to drain on kitchen paper.
6 Cut the meat in even pieces and serve with the mashed potatoes. Garnish with fresh thyme.

Findik ezmesi

Almond puree

250g (8.81oz)   almonds, peeled • 12 slices of white bread, crusts removed • 100ml (3.4fl.oz) milk • 2 cloves of garlic, squeezed • juice of 2 lemons • 4 tbsp olive oil • 1 tsp sea salt • black pepper • ½ tsp sugar • 2 tbsp parsley, finely chopped • 2 tbsp lemon balm, finely chopped

1 Soak the bread for 15 minutes in the milk. Squeeze the liquid out well.
2 Add the almonds, garlic and lemon juice.
3 Gradually mix the olive oil with a blender or food processor. Once it has turned into a cream, add salt, some pepper and the sugar to taste.
4 Add the parsley and lemon balm. Serve with hearty vegetables or pide bread.

Papaz Yahnisi

Stewed lamb in orange sauce

500g (1.10 lbs) lean lamb, in large blocks • 2 onions, in halved rings • 1-2 tbsp olive oil • 1-2 tbsp tomato puree • 3 cloves of garlic, peeled • 1 tsp cumin powder • 1 tsp allspice powder • strings pulled from the peel of half an orange • 3 bay leaves • pepper and salt

1 Put the meat with the onions in a pan and add some olive oil.
2 Mix the tomato puree with a bit of water and add the whole garlic cloves.
3 Pour the mixture with the meat and sprinkle with cumin and allspice and pepper and salt. Stir everything well.
4 Add the orange peel and bay leaves and put the pan covered with a lid on the hob. Bring to boil and leave to simmer for 30-40 minutes. Add water if it becomes too dry.
5 Remove the peels and the bay leaves before serving.

Havuç kavurması

Fried carrots in yoghurt-garlic sauce

4 medium-large carrots, scraped and in long thin strips • 3 tbsp olive oil • 2 tbsp Turkish yoghurt • 2-3 cloves of garlic, pounded to a paste in a mortar • 2 tbsp dried mint • salt • chilli flakes to taste

92

SHARP! Chilli flakes add some bite to dishes. They are often mixed with melted butter and used as a garnish. The flakes are made from the peel of dried red peppers.

1 Fry the carrots in a covered pan for 5-10 minutes in olive oil. Stir occasionally.
2 Mix the yoghurt with the garlic, mint, some salt and chilli flakes.
3 Take the carrots from the fire and add the yoghurt mixture. Serve as an appetizer.

Peynir salatası

Feta puree with parsley and cayenne

200g (7.05oz) white Turkish crumbly cheese (or feta) • 4 tbsp Turkish yoghurt (süzme) • 2 tbsp olive oil • 1 clove garlic, squeezed • 1 tbsp black pepper • ½ tsp cayenne pepper • 3 tbsp fresh parsley, finely chopped

CHEESE Turkish cheeses (peynir) are mainly short-ripened cheeses. They are mostly made from sheep or goat's milk sometimes mixed with cow's milk. Some cheeses are ripened in the skin of goats. In Turkish shops you can choose your own blocks of cheese kept in containers of salt water. You should also store this type of cheese in a bit of salt water home as this way it can be kept for about five days.

1 Mix all ingredients except the parsley in a blender or food processor.
2 Add the parsley.
3 Place in the fridge for about 8 hours so that the flavours can combine. Serve as an appetizer.

Kuru fasūlye

Rich bean soup with shoulder of lamb

150g (5.29oz) dried white beans, soaked for 8 hours in water • 250g (8.81oz)   lamb shoulder, in cubes • 2 onions, shredded • 2 tbsp olive oil • 2 ripe tomatoes, peeled, seeds removed and cut into cubes • 2 tsp tomato puree • 1 biber (sweet or sharp green paprika), seeds removed and in pieces • 400ml (13.5fl.oz) warm water • salt

96

1 Glaze the onions for 3 minutes in 1 tbsp oil and add the meat while constantly stirring. Turn the heat down to low and cover the pan with a lid.
2 Check if all the liquid from the meat has evaporated.
3 Add the tomatoes, tomato puree, biber, the rest of the oil and salt to taste.
4 Add enough warm water so that the meat is fully covered and cook until done (approximately 20 minutes) on a low flame.
5 Add the beans together with 800ml water. Bring to boil and leave to simmer for 1 hour on a low flame. (Take care that the beans do not burst This can happen when they are cooked for too long.)

TIP: Set the soup for aside a day as then it will taste even better. If the soup is too thick you can just add some water. You can also use chickpeas instead of beans. People in Turkey like to eat winter soup with raw onion and tursu.

İmam Bayıldı

Stuffed aubergine with tomato sauce

4 aubergines • For the stuffed: 3 white onions, in thin halved rings • 4 tbsp olive oil • 3 cloves of garlic, cut into small pieces • 1 biber (sweet or sharp paprika), seeds removed and in strips • 1 can of tomato cubes • 2 tbsp tomato puree • 1 tsp paprika puree or powder • 3 tbsp of fresh parsley, finely chopped • ½ tsp sea salt • ½ tsp black pepper • ½ tsp sugar • ¼ tsp nutmeg • 1 tomato, in pieces, for garnishing • 1 biber, in pieces, for garnishing • juice of ½ lemon

1 Cut the aubergines lengthwise without cutting them in two. Start about 2cm (0.8in) behind the stem until stop 2cm (0.8in) before the end.
2 Leave the aubergines to stand in salt water for 30 minutes. Rinse and dab them dry. Remove enough of the pulp until a 1cm layer remains. Set aside. Keep the hollowed aubergines.
3 Glaze the onions for 3 minutes in 1 tbsp oil and add the garlic and biber.
4 After 3 minutes add the tomatoes, tomato puree, paprika puree, parsley, salt, pepper, sugar, nutmeg and the aubergine pulp. Leave to simmer on a low flame for 25 minutes. Preheat the oven at 180°C (350F, Gas 4).
5 Put the hollowed aubergines in a greased oven dish and bake them for 10 minutes.
6 Fill the aubergines with the mixture. Put the tomato and biber on top. Sprinkle them with the rest of the olive oil and the lemon juice.
7 Put the leftover filling in the oven dish and add 100ml hot water. Cover with aluminium foil, put it back in the oven and leave the filled aubergines to cook in 45 minutes. Serve warm with pilav (see recipe on page 114).

98

FAINT Imam Bayildi is unmistakably the most famous Turkish vegetable dish. The name means 'the imam who felt faint'. The story has never clarified if this was due to pleasure or gluttony.

Köfte

Cumin-spiced minced meat

500g (1.10 lbs) minced lamb or beef • 3 slices of white bread, without crust (or 100g (3.52oz) ready-made breadcrumbs) • 2 onions, shredded • 2 cloves of garlic, squeezed • 2 tbsp cumin powder • 1 tbsp paprika powder • ½ tsp thyme • 1 tsp salt • ½ tsp black pepper • 3 tbsp olive oil • 3 tomatoes, in slices.

100

SPECIALTY Köfte, just, like kebab one of the specialties of the Turkish kitchen. The name köfte has more to do with the form than the way it is prepared, because the minced meat rods can be eaten fried, deep-fried, steamed as well as raw. Normal köftes are as big as a thumb, while filled köftes look more like a top. They are a very popular dinner dish and are served in great amounts on large plates.

1 Soak the bread in water and squeeze it out.
2 Mix the minced meat with the bread, the onions, garlic, cumin, paprika, thyme, the salt and the pepper.
3 Knead well and make rods (köfte) roughly the the size of a thumb only thicker.
4 Heat the olive oil and fry the köfte light brown.
5 Leave the slices of tomato on the köfte and sprinkle them with some salt. Cover the pan, turn the flame low and leave everything for 10 minutes until it is done. Serve with pilav (see recipe on page 114), pide (bread, see recipe elsewhere in book) or bulgur wheat.

Örülmüş tavuk

Chicken and courgettes in tomato sauce

500 g chicken fillet, in large pieces • 1 onion, shredded • 3 tbsp olive oil • 2 tomatoes, seeds removed and in cubes • 200 ml warm water 2 big courgettes, in long thin slices • 1 fleshy tomato, in slices • 2 bibers (sweet or sharp green paprikas), seeds removed and in big pieces • 4 twigs of parsley, coarsely cut • pepper and salt • 8 wooden cocktail sticks

1 Glaze for the sauce the onion in 1 tbsp of olive oil. Add the tomatoes and leave to simmer for 5 minutes on a low fire. Pour some water in and leave to simmer gently for another 5-10 minutes. Add salt and pepper to taste.
2 Preheat the oven on 190°C (375, Gas 5).
3 Bake the courgette strips golden brown in the rest of the oil and leave to drain on kitchen paper.
4 Put 2 slices of courgette crossed on a plate. On the middle put a piece of chicken fillet and fold the ends of the courgette towards each other. Put a slice of tomato on top and then a piece of biber. Sprinkle with some salt and pepper.
5 Fasten with a cocktail stick and put in a greased oven dish. Repeat with the rest of the pieces of meat.
6 Pour the tomato sauce in the oven dish, but not over the packages. Sprinkle the sauce with parsley. Pour extra hot water in it if the bottom of the dish is not completely covered in sauce.
7 Cover with the aluminium foil and leave in the oven for 45 minutes until well done. Serve warm.

VARIATION Instead of chicken, use the same amount of lean beef and use strips of aubergine instead of courgette. Leave for an hour in the oven.

Etli bamya

Okra with lamb

250g (8.81oz)   lamb (preferably leg of lamb), in cubes • 500g (1.10 lbs) fresh okras (or 250g(8.81oz)   dried okra) • 2 tbsp butter • 1 onion, cut small • 2 tbsp tomato puree • 200ml (6.8 fl.oz) water • juice of 1 lemon • pepper and salt

LADIES Okra is a long, ribbed vegetable the size of a finger and is also known as lady's finger. It functions as a thickener in dishes and when it is cooked it looks a bit slimy. The taste, however, is wonderful. Outside of the season okra is available in dried form (threaded on a string) or in a can. Remove the dried okras from the string with a cloth.

1   Cut the stems from the fresh okras, making sure to keep 2mm of the stem on the vegetable. Carefully cut away the brown ridge around the head in a diagonal cut, not a straight cut. Wash the okras well and cook them for 3-5 minutes in 1 litre of water. Drain and keep in the water used to boil them.
2   Fry the meat gently for 10 minutes in 1 tbsp of butter and cover the pan.
3   Mix the onion, 1 tbsp butter and the tomato puree with meat. Add salt to taste.
4   Pour in 200ml water and bring to the boil. Cover the pan and leave to simmer for 30 minutes.
5   Add the okras, the okra cooking liquid, the lemon juice and some black pepper. Leave to simmer for another 30-40 minutes. Serve warm with pilav (see recipe on page 114).

Alinazik

Minced veal with aubergine puree

500g (1.10 lbs) minced veal (or lean minced beef) • 3 aubergines • juice of 1 lemon • 3 cloves of garlic, squeezed • 5 tbsp yoghurt (süzme) • 1 tbsp butter • 1 tsp chilli flakes • 4 bibers (sweet or sharp green paprikas) grilled • 4 slices of tomato, grilled • pepper and salt • oil

1 Pierce the aubergines on to a fork and hold them directly above a gas flame. Rotate them slowly until they are well done.
2 Leave them to rest for 20 minutes in a closed plastic bag. The peel will then easily come loose. Remove the blackened peel. Plunge the aubergines in water, rub them in with lemon juice and rinse them again.
3 Mash the aubergines until fine and then mix the puree with the garlic, pepper and salt.
4 Spice the minced meat with pepper and salt and fry for 2-5 minutes on a low flame in some oil.
5 Portion the aubergine puree on to the plates and spread thinly. Scoop on a layer of yoghurt then a layer of mince on top of that.
6 Melt the butter with the chilli flakes and heat for 2 minutes. Sprinkle the sauce over the dish. Garnish with grilled biber and tomato.

TIP: you can also bake the aubergine in the oven.Pierce the pulp a few times with a fork and cook for one hour on the highest setting.

NAME The name of this dish roughly translates to 'Ali the gentleman.'.

Zeytinyağlı fasulye

French beans in tomato sauce

500g (1.10 lbs) French beans • 2 tbsp olive oil • 1 onion, shredded • 2 cloves of garlic, in thin slices • 4 ripe tomatoes, in cubes • 2 tbsp tomato puree • 4 tbsp parsley, finely chopped • 2 tsp sugar • 1 tsp sea salt • ½ tsp black pepper

1 Heat the French beans briefly in 1 tbsp oil until it changes colour.
2 Glaze the onion in a big pan in 1 tbsp oil and add the garlic.
3 Add tomato, tomato puree, parsley, sugar, salt and pepper and leave to boil for 5 minutes.
4 Put half of the French beans in a pan and pour as much tomato mixture over it so that the beans are covered. Put the rest of the beans on top and pour the rest of the sauce over it.
5 Add some water so that the beans are just covered. Lower the heat, remove the lid and leave the beans to simmer for 1 hour. Leave to cool in the sauce.

Barbunya buğulaması

Red gurnard with split pea puree

1 kilo red gurnard, cleaned • 4 tomatoes, cut small • 3 onions, shredded • 6 twigs of parsley, finely chopped • 6 bay leaves • juice of 2 lemons • 2 tbsp olive oil • pepper and salt, to taste • 1 lemon, for garnishing • For the pea puree: 250g (8.81oz) split peas • 2 tbsp olive oil • 1 onion, shredded • 500ml (17fl.oz) water • 2 tsp lemon juice • 2 tsp sugar • ½ tsp sea salt • ½ tsp black pepper • white wine (optional)

1 Soak the peas over night in water.
2 Marinate the fish in an oven dish with the tomatoes, onions, parsley, bay leaves, the lemon juice, the oil, pepper and salt. White wine can also be added to the marinade (optional). Cover with aluminium foil and leave to cool for several hours.
3 Heat for the pea puree 1 tbsp olive oil and glaze the onion in this. Add the water.
4 Bring to boil and add the peas, 1 tsp lemon juice, the sugar and the salt. Leave to simmer for an hour until the peas are almost bursting.
5 In the meantime preheat the oven for 180°C (350F, Gas 4). Put the fish in the oven and leave to bake for 15-20 minutes. Check once in a while to see if it needs more water.
6 Mash the peas in a blender or a food processor. Sprinkle with the rest of the lemon juice, 1 tbsp olive oil and the black pepper. Serve the fish with the pea puree and lemon slices.

110

TIP: this meal is also nice with mul (red mullet), a fish that is best eaten at the end of the summer.

Safran soslu jumbo karidesi

Shrimps in saffron sauce

500g (1.10 lbs) large shrimps, peeled • 350g (12.34oz) pasta to choice • 4 saffron threads • 3 tbsp kaymak (or fresh cream), thinned with water until it becomes 125ml (0.37fl.oz) • 1 tsp black pepper • black olives • 3 tbsp olive oil

EXTRA CREAMY Kaymak is a kind of thick cream that is sold in the Turkish shop. You can also easily make it yourself: gently heat some cream in a small pan for 20 minutes. Use a decent amount of cream because it thickens very quickly. Remove from heat and allow to cool. A yellow crust will form and underneath that will be thick, stiff cream.

1 Cook the pasta.
2 Heat the saffron with the kaymak and black pepper for 1 minute on a low heat.
3 Mix the pasta with the sauce and stir well.
4 Fry the shrimps and olives for 2 minutes on a high heat. Take them out of the pan and serve warm with the pasta.

Şiş kebap ve pilav

Lambs skewers with pilav

500g (1.10 lbs) sliced lamb • 1 tsp black pepper • 2 tsp sea salt • 100g (3.52oz) rocket • 2 tomatoes, thinly cut • 1 white onion, in thin rings • For the marinade: juice of 2 lemons • 2 onions, shredded • 2 cloves of garlic, squeezed • 2 twigs of thyme, finely chopped • 3 tbsp fresh parsley, finely chopped • 5 tbsp olive oil • For the pilav: 200g (7.05oz) long grain rice, washed • 2 tbsp barley (arpa sehriye) • 2 tbsp butter • 400ml (13.5fl.oz) broth or cold water • salt to taste.

114

PILAV In almost every lokanta, this pilav, with its characteristic barley grains, is served with the meal. The barley (arpa) can often be found in the same area as the pasta in Turkish shops. Use a wooden spoon during preparation and be careful not to break the grains of rice. Melted butter is almost always added to rice in order to enhance the flavour. The amount of butter depends on personal preference. The rice is allowed to settle for a time before being served. A lot of Turkish dishes are served lukewarm because that is when the taste is at its best.

1 Rub the lamb with pepper and salt.
2 Mix the ingredients for the marinade. Marinate the meat in this for at least 2 hours; the ideal marinating time is about 8 hours. After that, thread the slices of meat on the skewers.
3 Leave the rice to soak for 30 minutes in lukewarm salt water and then leave it to drain.
4 Fry the barley grains in 1 tbsp butter on a medium flame until they are light brown. Add the broth and salt and bring to the boil.
5 Mix the rice through it and put a lid on the pan. Leave on low heat until all liquid has been absorbed.
6 Melt the leftover butter and pour it over the rice. Remove from the heat and leave the closed pan to rest for another 10 minutes.
7 Grill or roast the meat on the skewers on as hot a heat as possible, taking care that the meat still remains a little pink. Garnish with rocket, tomato and onion. Serve with the pilav.

Tavuk ve bezelyeli pilav

Chicken fillets with peas and rice

2 chicken fillets with skin, halved • 2 tbsp fresh thyme leaves • 1 tbsp paprika puree • 1 tsp black pepper, grinded • 1 tsp salt • 3 tbsp olive oil • a few twigs of thyme • For the rice with peas: 200g (7.05oz) Turkish rice, rinsed • 300 g meat broth or cold water • 3 tbsp butter • 100g (3.52oz) peas, cooked and drained • salt

1 Preheat the oven at 180°C (350F, Gas 4). Mix the thyme leaves, paprika puree, pepper and salt with olive oil.
2 Rub the meat with the herb mixture. Put a few thyme twigs under the skin.
3 Bake the chicken for 1 hour golden brown in the oven.
4 In the meantime leave the rice to soak in lukewarm salt water and leave it to drain.
5 Bring the rice to the boil in the broth and add some salt. Turn the heat down to low and leave to cook until all the liquid is absorbed.
6 Melt 2 tbsp butter and pour over the rice. Remove from heat, cover and leave to rest for another 10 minutes.
7 Melt in another pan the rest of the butter and stir the peas through. Mix them with the rice. Serve the rice with the chicken.

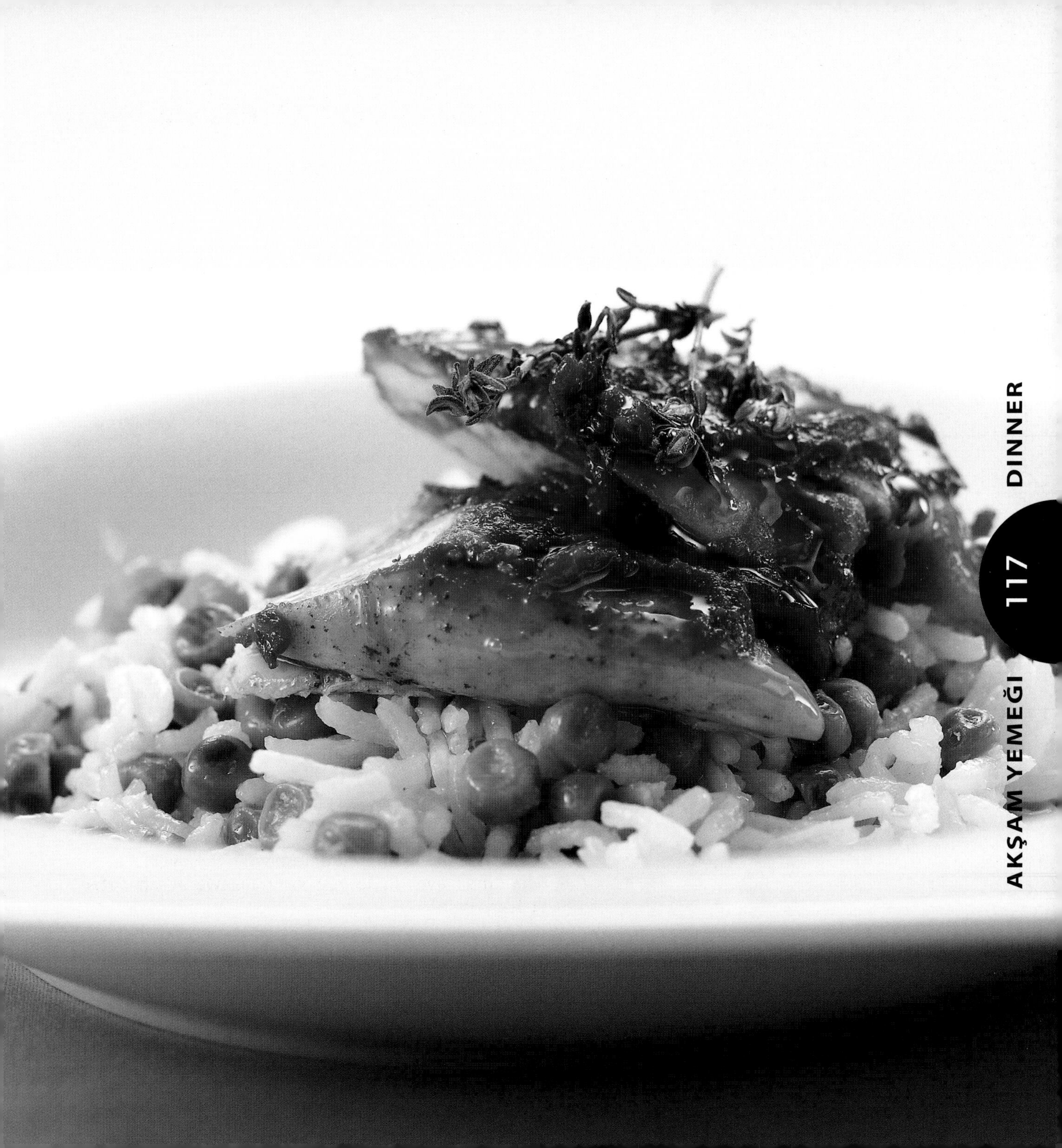

118

SHINY RED The pomegranate has a red, shiny leathery peel and a crown with six lips on the bottom. The juice form the basis of grenadine) and the sweet pulp is used in desserts. The numerous brown black seeds are used in salads or in dishes like köfte. When the ripe fruit falls from the tree, the seeds scatter in all directions – that is why the hand grenade is named after this apple.

Bitlis köftesi ve bulgur pilavı

Pomegranate meatballs with bulgur pilav

200g (7.05oz) lean minced beef • 100g (3.52oz) pomegranate pips • 2 onions, cut small • 2 tbsp olive oil • 50g rice, rinsed • 100ml (3.4fl.oz) water (for the rice) • 1 tsp salt (for the rice) • 1 tsp black pepper • 200g (7.05oz) ince bulgur (fine bulgur) • 100ml (3.4fl.oz) water (for the bulgur) • 1 tsp salt (for the bulgur) • 1 egg • For the bulgur pilav: 2 cups coarse bulgur, washed • 2 onions, shredded • 2 tbsp butter • 2 ripe tomatoes, peeled and in cubes • 600ml (20.3fl.oz) meat broth or lukewarm water • salt and black pepper

1 Fry the onions for 5 minutes in the oil.
2 Place the rice, 100ml of water and the salt into the pan. Leave to cook for 15 minutes on a low flame.
3 Take the rice off the heat and add the pomegranate pips and the pepper.
4 In the meantime pour 100ml hot water with salt on the fine bulgur and leave to rest for 15 minutes.
5 Add mince, the egg and a bit more salt and knead in 10 minutes till you get a smooth mass. Wet your hands and roll into balls the size of walnuts.
6 Make a hole in each ball. Fill this with the rice pomegranate pip mixture and make sure to close the edges well. Make oval shapes by rolling both sides into a point.
7 Steam it for 25 minutes till done in a steamer. Alternatively, you can hang a colander in a pan above some boiling water. Make sure to put a lid over the colander.
8 To make the pilav, glaze the onions for about 3 minutes in 1 tbsp butter. Add the bulgur and stir until the butter is absorbed.
9 Add the tomatoes and stir until all cooking liquid is absorbed.
10 Pour the broth in and bring to the boil. Leave for 10-15 minutes to cook gently. Remove from the heat from the moment all the liquid has been absorbed. Bring to taste with salt and black pepper.
11 Melt remaining butter and pour it over Bulgur. Leave for 5 minutes before serving.

Cevizli havuç salatası

Carrot-walnut salad

500g (1.10 lbs) carrots, grated • 125g (4.40oz) walnuts, finely chopped • 3 tbsp olive oil • 1 tsp paprika puree or powder • 2 tbsp cumin • ½ tsp black pepper • 1 tsp sea salt • 2 cloves of garlic pounded into a paste with a mortar • 100ml (3.4fl.oz) Turkish yoghurt (süzme) • 2 tbsp fresh parsley, finely chopped

1 Heat the olive oil and fry the carrots for 3 minutes.
2 Add the walnuts, paprika puree, cumin, black pepper and the salt. Fry again for 3 minutes and leave to cool.
3 In the meantime mix the garlic through the yoghurt. Scoop this mixture through the carrots. Serve with parsley.

Terbiyeli köfte ve zeytinyağlı pırasa

Minced meat in lemon sauce with leek and rice

500g (1.10 lbs) minced meat • 3 slices of white bread • 2 onions, finely cut • 2 tbsp fresh parsley, finely cut • ½ tsp black pepper • 1 tsp sea salt • 3 tsp flour • 350 ml water • 2 winter carrots, in cubes • 2 big potatoes, in cubes • 1 egg yolk • 1½ tbsp lemon juice • For the leek and rice: 1 kg (2.2lbs) leeks, diagonally cut into pieces of 3-5cm • 8 tbsp olive oil • 1 winter carrot, in large strips • 3-4 cloves of garlic, pressed • 2 tbsp rice, washed • 3 tbsp parsley, finely chopped • ½ tsp sugar • ½ tsp black pepper • ½ tsp sea salt • juice of one lemon

1 Soak the bread in cold water and squeeze the water out. Mix the bread with the minced meat, onions, parsley and pepper and salt.
2 Knead for 5 minutes and make balls the size of a walnut. Roll the meatballs in the flour until completely covered.
3 Boil the water with some salt in a large pan. Cook the meatballs in this for 45 minutes on a low flame with the pan covered.
4 After 30 minutes add the carrot and potato.
5 In the meantime make the leek and rice. Heat the oil and fry the leek, carrot and garlic for 15 minutes.
6 Add the rice and 2 tbsp parsley. Add sugar, pepper and salt to taste.
7 Add some water and cover the pan with a lid. Leave to cook gently for 10 minutes. Turn the off the heat and leave to rest for another 10 minutes. Remove the garlic.
8 Set aside to cool and sprinkle with some ground pepper, the rest of the parsley and the lemon juice.
9 For the sauce, whisk the egg yolk through the lemon juice. Stir 3 tbsp of the cooking liquid of the meatballs through. Pour this in the pan constantly stirring and boil for 2 minutes until the sauce becomes thick. Serve with the leek and rice.

Kabak tatlısı

Pumpkin with cream and walnuts

1kg (2.2lbs) pumpkin • 250g (8.81oz) sugar • 2 tbsp walnuts , chopped • kaymak (or fresh cream) to taste

124

1   Remove the peel and seeds of the pumpkin. Cut the flesh into long strips.
2   Boil the pumpkin until it is cooked or until most of the water has evaporated.
3   Then add the sugar and slowly boil down until it turns into a syrup. Take care that the pumpkin pieces do not start to stick together.
4   Leave the pumpkin to cool off in the syrup. Serve cold with chopped walnuts and kaymak.

TIP: Do not throw away the white pumpkin seeds because they are very healthy. Once dried and roasted, they can be eaten as a snack or added to a salad.

Limonlu dondurma

Lemon sorbet

300ml (10.2fl.oz) water with a few drops of lemon juice • 100g (3.52oz) sugar • grated peel of 1 lemon • juice of 3 lemons, sieved • ½ egg white, whisked • 1 leafy twig of mint • pistachio nuts, chopped, for garnishing

1 Boil the water with the sugar and lemon peel for 5 minutes.
2 Add the lemon juice and leave to cool off. Pour into an airtight container and place in the freezer.
3 Turn the freezer setting to high. Check after a while if the ice has begun to form. Once it has formed, then stir the mixture well.
4 Add a bit of the egg white and put the sorbet back in the freezer.
5 Stir occasionally. Put the freezer stand to normal when the sorbet is thick enough (in approximately 5 hours). Garnish with mint leaves and pistachio nuts.

Muz likörü

Banana liqueur

500g (1.10 lbs) bananas • brandy • white sugar

AFTER DINNER If you want to end your meal on a high note, then you should serve Turkish coffee, a piece of lokum (Turkish delight) and a glass of liqueur. Simply delicious!

1 Mash the bananas and scoop them in a pot with a lid.
2 Pour in enough brandy so that the tops of the bananas are just covered. Leave to stand for 3-4 days.
3 Sieve the contents of the pot so that the brandy becomes yellow.
4 Measure an amount of sugar that is equal to the amount of brandy.
5 Bring the sugar with an equal amount of water to the boil. Leave to boil down until it becomes a syrup. Add the syrup to the alcohol mixture and sieve everything. Keep the sieved liquid in a closed bottle.

Ziyafet yemekleri

Ezo Gelin çorbası

Bride´s soup

1 onion, shredded • 2 tbsp butter • 2 tbsp tomato puree or 2 ripe tomatoes • ½ tsp paprika puree • 1l water • 100g (3.52oz) red or yellow lentils, washed • 100g (3.52oz) ince bulgur (fine bulgur) • 2 tsp mint • 2 tsp paprika powder • salt and pepper

PRETTY LADY This Turkish tomato soup with lentils is named after Ezo Gelin, a very beautiful lady who was born in 1909 in the Gaziantep province. Several films have been made about her life. The soup used to mainly be served for wedding banquets in the country. Nowadays it is available everywhere.

1 Glaze the onion in 1 tbsp butter until it is light brown.
2 Stir the tomato and paprika puree during 1-2 minutes with a wooden spoon.
3 Pour the water in and bring to boil. Add the lentils, bulgur and salt and pepper.
4 Simmer for one hour to allow all ingredients to cook thoroughly.
5 Blend with a hand-held blender.
6 Melt 1 tbsp butter and mix with the mint and paprika powder. Garnish the soup with it and serve immediately.

Sıgara böreği

Cheese horns

500g (1.10 lbs) yufka (the triangular sheets) • 300g (10.58oz) white cheese (or feta) • 100g (3.52oz) Turkish yoghurt (süzme) • 4 tbsp verse dill, finely chopped • 4 tbsp fresh parsley, finely chopped • 1 egg • flour • pepper and salt • olive oil

1 Mix the cheese, yoghurt, herbs and the egg. Add pepper and salt to taste.
2 Thaw the dough and work it quickly so that it does not dry out.
3 Sprinkle the workspace with flour. Spread the cheese mix on the dough slices (make sure the layer is not too thick) and roll them up until they have a cigar form. Wet the edges and press down well.
4 Heat some olive oil and fry the rolls until they are golden brown. Leave them to drain on kitchen paper. Serve them with a glass of tea, as snack or as appetizers. They will also taste good if served the following day.

134

TIP: If you cannot find yufka dough pre-cut into triangles, then simply cut the required pieces from large sheets of yufka.

Zeytinyağlı yaprak sarması

Stuffed wine leaves with herbed rice

250g (8.81oz) pickled wine leaves (about 40 pieces), soaked for 1 hour in water • 200g (7.05oz) long grain rice • 150ml (5.1fl.oz) olive oil • 2 onions, shredded • 2 tbsp tomato puree • 2 tomatoes, finely cut • ½ tsp cinnamon • ½ tsp sugar • 250ml (8.5fl.oz) water • juice of 1 lemon • 3 tbsp parsley, finely chopped • 2 tbsp dill, finely chopped • 2 tbsp mint, finely chopped • pepper and salt • 1 lemon, for garnishing • yoghurt

1 Rinse the wine leaves a few times with water and boil them for 5 minutes. Rinse again and set aside to cool.
2 Heat some olive oil and glaze the shredded onion with half of the tomato puree and the tomatoes.
3 Add the rice, cinnamon, sugar and pepper and salt. Stir for 2 minutes until the rice is glassy.
4 Add water. Leave to simmer for 15 minutes until all water is absorbed.
5 Add the largest part of the lemon juice and the herbs.
6 Cover the bottom of a pan with some wine leaves.
7 Lay a wine leaf down on the workspace with the veins facing upwards and remove the stem. Scoop 1-2 tsp filling along the width of the leaf. Fold the beginning of the stem over it and then both sides. Next roll the sarma tightly so that it is roughly the size of a little finger. Repeat with the rest of the wine leaves.
8 Put a few of the rolls veined-side down on the wine leaves in the pan. Sprinkle with some lemon juice and olive oil and put another layer on top.
9 Add the rest of the tomato puree and enough water that everything is covered. Put something heavy on the sarmas (such as a plate or lid) and bring to the boil.
10 Leave to simmer for 1 hour. Take care that the pan does not dry out. Leave the sarma to cool in the liquid. Serve with pieces of lemon and thick whole yoghurt.

VARIATION You can leave out the tomato puree and use 110g (3.88oz) pine nuts and 100g raisins for the filling instead.

Çiğ köfte

Minced meat rolls

500g (1.10 lbs) lean beef mince • 3 large onions, shredded • 1 tbsp tomato puree • 1 tbsp paprika puree or powder • cumin powder to taste • allspice powder to taste• 200g (7.05oz) çig köftelik bulgur (fine and granular), soaked in hot water for 30 minutes • 5 twigs of parsley, coarsely chopped • salt and pepper • For garnishing: 3 onions, shredded • 5 twigs of parsley, coarsely chopped • salt • cumin powder to taste• allspice powder to taste • 2 tbsp sharp paprika puree (or chilli flakes) • lemon juice • olive oil

KNEADING Knead the minced meat by hand and without mercy! As the Turkish saying goes: 'Whosoever is the strongest, kneads the minced meat.'

1 Mix the onions through the mince.
2 Knead well and add tomato puree, paprika puree, cumin, allspice powder and salt and pepper.
3 Add the bulgur and knead vigorously for 10 minutes. Add some drops of water while kneading, but not too much.
4 Place some parsley in your palm and then form a meatball the size of a thumb. Repeat.
5 Place the rolls on a large dish (with the garnish placed around the rolls) so that guests can help themselves.

Dürüm-partisi (sac)

Dip bread

1kg (2.2lbs) flour • 20g (0.70oz) dried yeast (or baker's yeast) • 2 tsp salt • 4-5 tbsp lukewarm water • 2 tbsp olive oil • extra flour for the work space

140

ROLLING AND DIPPING
In Turkey everyone rolls pieces of this paper-thin bread into cones and fills them with prefer. The bread is served on a big, round, metal serving plate (the tepsi) with diverse sauces and small dishes, such as different mini-köftes, small pieces of vegetables, aubergine puree, humus, and almond sauce. The filled cones can be dipped in aromatic olive oil, pepper flake butter and cacik (yoghurt-cucumber sauce). Dürüm is also pre-packed for sale. If pressed for time, one can make 'wraps' and cut them in pieces of 10 by 10cm (3.9ins).

1 Mix the flour with the yeast and the salt. Add the lukewarm water drop by drop.
2 Pour the olive oil in and knead for 10 minutes until it becomes a smooth dough. Leave this to rise for 30 minutes under a wet towel.
3 Knead the dough again. With the help of a long wooden stick (such as the handle of a wooden spoon) roll very thin crepes on a workspace that has been covered with flour.
4 Heat a cast iron crêpe pan or a broad heavy pan. Fry the bread on both sides until it is dry. Leave it to form bubbles, but make sure it stays flexible.
5 Keep the fried bread (sac) under a towel until everything else has been fried. Cut the bread into squares of 10x10 cm and serve with several different side dishes and sauces.

Barbunya fasulyesi

Kidney been salad

1kg (2.2lbs) kidney beans or brown beans, cooked • 1 white onion or 2 shallots, shredded • 1 fleshy tomato, seeds removed and in small pieces • 1 small potato, in cubes • 1 small carrot, in fine cubes • 6 cloves of garlic, in slices • 5 tbsp olive oil • 1 tsp sugar • 2 tsp salt • 2 cups of water • ½ lemon, in slices • ½ lemon, in quarters, for garnishing • 6 twigs parsley, for garnishing

1   Remove any hard pieces of skin from the beans.
2   Bring all ingredients to the boil except those that are for garnishing.
3   Leave to simmer for 1 hour covered with a lid on a low temperature.
4   Leave to cool and after that put it in the fridge until the dish is completely cool. Garnish with parsley and lemon. Serve as an appetizer or side dish.

Etli dolmalar

Stuffed vegetables with spicy minced meat

2 large courgettes with peel, in pieces of 7-8cm (2.8ins-3.1ins) • 4 medium-large tomatoes, remove cap • 6 bibers (green Turkish paprika's), remove cap and seeds removed • 250g (8.81oz) minced veal or beef • 4 tbsp olive oil • 100g (3.52oz) rice, washed • 2 onions, shredded • 4 tbsp parsley, finely chopped • 4 tbsp dill, finely chopped • 1 tsp dried mint • 2 cloves of garlic, squeezed • ½ tsp cumin • ½ tsp all spice • pepper and salt

TIP: Stuffed vegetables taste even better the following day! Keep them under a layer of olive oil in the fridge. You can also make this meal in the oven. Leave the vegetables to cook for about 1hour at 180°C (350F, Gas 4). Put some mashed white cheese on top. You can use the courgette pulp to make courgette puff-pancakes (see following recipe).

1. Remove alternate lengths of peel from the outside of the courgettes so the result is a pattern of stripes.
2. Hollow out the insides, but leave the bottom intact.
3. Scoop out the pulp from the tomatoes and set aside.
4. Firmly stir the mince with 3 tbsp of olive oil, the rice, onion, parsley, dill, mint, garlic and half of the tomato pulp. Also add cumin, allspice and pepper and salt and leave for a few minutes to settle.
5. Stuff the courgettes, tomatoes and bibers with the filling until they are about two-thirds full.
6. Put the courgettes and paprikas in a big pan next to each other. Put the tomatoes on top as a second layer.
7. Pour what is left of the olive oil and the tomato pulp in the pan. Add the water until it is half full.
8. Cover the pan with a lid, gradually bring to boil and leave to simmer for 30 minutes. Check if the vegetables are cooked. Allow to cool.

Kabaklı mücver

Small courgette puff-pancakes

2 courgettes, grated• 75g (2.64oz) flour • 75g (2.64oz) Turkish white cheese or feta, crumbled • 3 eggs, whisked • 1 large onion, shredded • 2 tbsp butter • 6 tbsp dill, finely chopped • pepper and salt • olive oil

1 Add the flour with some pepper and salt to the cheese.
2 Mix the eggs through.
3 Glaze the onion for 2 minutes in the butter. Add the grated courgettes and the dill and fry for 2 minutes.
4 Separate the solid food from any liquid that may have escaped from the vegetables during cooking. Scoop the solid mixture into a dish with the batter. Mix well.
5 Heat the olive oil in a frying pan. Scoop spoonfuls of the batter in the pan with some space in between. Fry the puff-pancakes on both sides until they are cooked and golden brown.
6 Leave them to drain on a bit of kitchen paper and serve them warm. Serve with cacik (yoghurt cucumber sauce; see recipe on page 76).

Ispanaklı içli köfte

Filled wheat köfte with spinach mince and walnuts

500g (1.10 lbs) icli köftelik bulgur (very fine grain) • 2-3 tbsp semolina • 1 egg • salt • water • For the filling: 2 large onions, shredded • 2 tbsp butter • 150g (5.29oz) minced meat • 100g (3.52oz) spinach, blanched and finely chopped • 1 tbsp walnuts, finely chopped • a pinch of cinnamon • pinch of allspice • pepper and salt • For the sauce: 2 tbsp olive oil • 2 tbsp tomato puree (or 3 ripe tomatoes) • 50ml water • 2 cloves of garlic, pounded into a paste in a mortar

1. Mix the bulgur, semolina, egg and salt in a bowl. Knead for 5-10 minutes so that the ingredients are well combined.
2. Add the water drop by drop until the dough is smooth, stirring all the while.
3. For the filling, glaze the onions in the butter and add the minced meat. Stir for 2-3 minutes. Then add the spinach with the walnuts, cinnamon and allspice. Add pepper and salt to taste.
4. Put some dough (an amount the size of an egg) in your palm. Press flat and fill with ½ tbsp of the minced meat mixture. Press the dough closed. Repeat with the rest of the dough and the filling, moistening your hands every once in a while.
5. Bring some water with salt to the boil and put in the 'dough eggs'. Leave them for a very short time to cook on a low temperature. Keep the cooking water to use as a thickener for soups.
6. In the meantime, make the sauce. Heat the olive oil and stir the tomato puree, the water and the garlic through. Serve the köfte warm with the sauce.

İzmir köftesi

Köfte minced meat

400g (14oz) minced beef or lamb • piece of pide (flat bread) • 1 egg • 1 onion, shredded • 1 tbsp cumin seed • 2 tbsp flour • 2 tbsp olive oil • 1 green dolmalik biber, or green paprika, in strips • 2 cloves of garlic, pressed • 1 can peeled tomatoes • 1 tsp sugar • 3 tbsp fresh parsley, finely chopped • pepper and salt

1 Soak the bread in some water and squeeze out the liquid.
2 Combine the minced meat, the egg, the onion, cumin seeds, pepper and salt and knead well.
3 Make them into balls and roll through the flour until thoroughly covered.
4 Heat the olive oil in a frying pan and fry the mince rolls until brown. Remove from the pan.
5 Fry the paprika and garlic in the same pan and add the peeled tomatoes. Add the sugar, pepper and salt to taste.

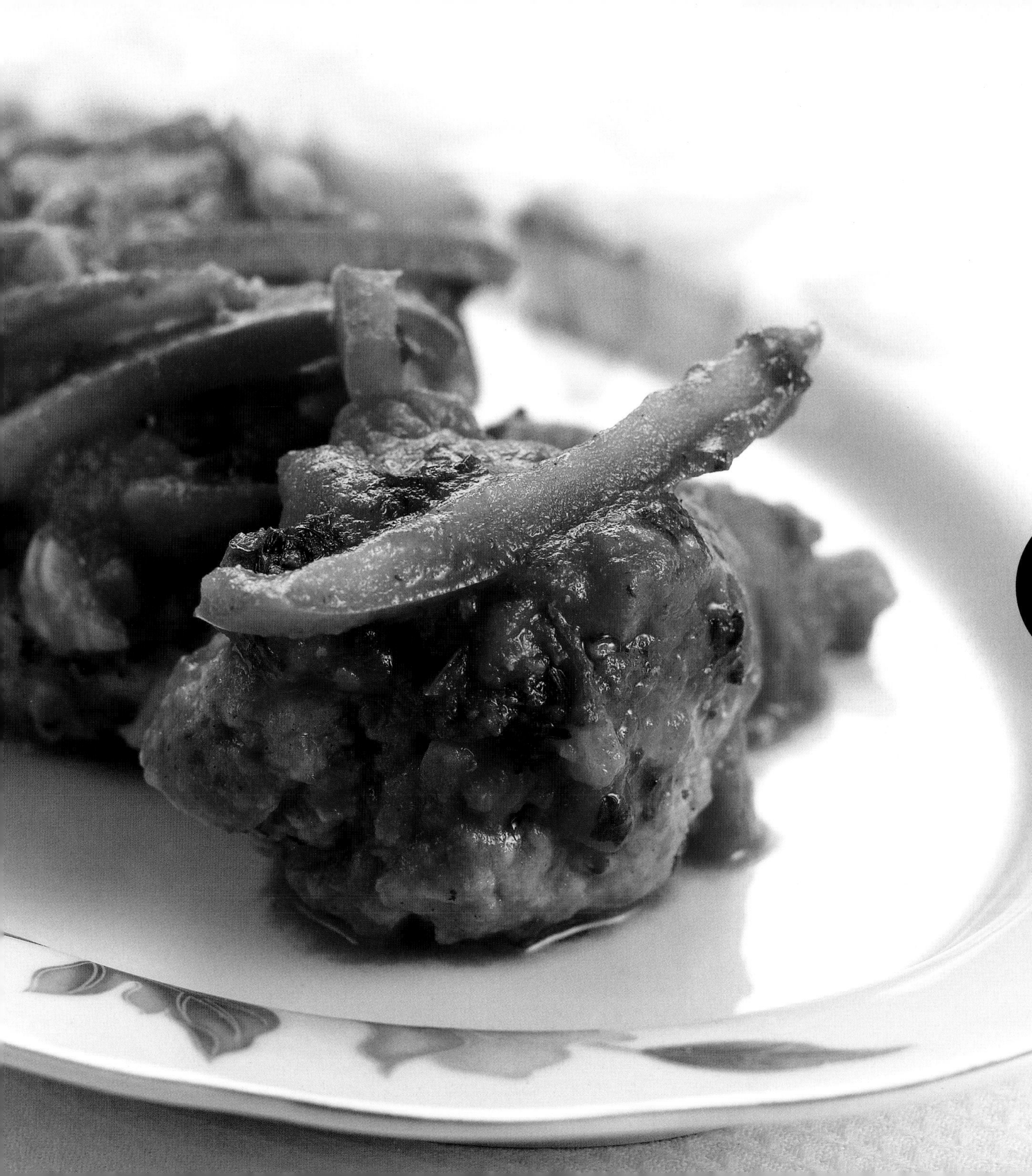

Hünkârbeğendi

Shoulder of lamb with cheese-aubergine puree

500g (1.10 lbs) shoulder lamb without bone, in pieces • 1 onion, shredded • 1 tbsp butter • 1 tomato, peeled and in cubes • 150 ml hot water • pepper and salt • For the sauce: 2 large aubergines • 150ml (5.1fl.oz) lemon juice, mixed with cold water • 1 tbsp flour • 50 g butter • 150ml (5.1fl.oz) milk • 50g (1.76oz) cheese, grated • ½ tsp salt • ½ tsp pepper • 2 twigs mint, for garnishing

1. Heat the meat with the onion and butter in a covered pan. Allow the liquid from the meat to evaporate.
2. Add the tomato with some pepper and salt and leave to boil for 5 minutes. Then add the water and leave the meat to cook for 30-45 minutes.
3. In the meantime grill the aubergines for about 30 minutes directly in a gas flame or for 1 hour in the oven on 220°C (425F, Gas 7).
4. Remove the blackened skin and leave the aubergines for a while in the lemon juice with water. Then press the liquid out, cut the pips away if necessary, and mash the aubergines.
5. Fry the flour with half of the butter for 2-3 minutes. Add the milk drop by drop and the mashed aubergines.
6. Leave to cook for 5-10 minutes. Take from the hob and add the cheese, the rest of the butter, the salt and the pepper.
7. Heat the puree for another 6-8 minutes au bain-marie.
8. Portion the puree on to the plates. Make a hole in each serving of puree in which the meat is placed. Garnish with mint and serve with pilav (see recipe on page 114).

POETRY The literal translation of the name of the this dish is 'majesty's joy'. Turkish dishes originating from the courts of the Ottoman empire often received the most beautiful, poetic names, such the desserts known as 'navel of the lady' and 'lips of lovers'.

Kılıç şiş

Grilled swordfish

500g (1.10 lbs) swordfish, in cubes • 4 solid fleshy tomatoes, in pieces • 1 onion, in pieces • 4 dolmalik bibers, or green paprikas, in pieces • 1 lemon, in slices • radishes, in slices • some twigs parsley, chopped • a bit of olive oil • For the marinade: 2 tbsp olive oil • 5-6 bay leaves • 1 onion, shredded • 2 tbsp lemon juice • pepper and salt

1 Mix the ingredients for the marinade. Marinate the fish for a minimum of 3 hours, although the preferred marinating time is 8 hours.
2 Preheat the oven at 180°C (350F, Gas 4) or turn on the barbeque. Thread the fish, tomato, onion and biber on to the skewers.
3 Grill the skewers for 10-15 minutes in the oven or for about 5 minutes on the barbeque. Garnish with slices of lemon, radishes, parsley and some olive oil.

Mercimekli köfte

Lentil-bulgur balls

200g (7.05oz) red lentils, washed • 500ml (17fl.oz) water • 150g (5.29oz) ince bulgur (fine bulgur), washed • 2 tbsp butter • 3 onions, shredded • 2 tomatoes, finely cut or 1 tbsp tomato puree • 3 tbsp olive oil • 3 bibers (sharp or sweet green paprika), cut into small pieces • 1 bunch of spring onions, cut into small pieces • 4-6 twigs parsley, finely chopped • cumin powder • chilli flakes • pepper and salt • endive leaves, for garnishing

1. Cook the lentils in the water until all the liquid is absorbed.
2. Take the pan off the hob, add the bulgur and some salt and cover with a lid or plate. Leave to stand for 10 minutes, so that the bulgur can expand.
3. Melt the butter and glaze the onions for 2-3 minutes. Add the tomatoes and fry them for a minute.
4. Put the onions and tomatoes with the lentils. Also add the olive oil, bibers, spring onions and parsley. Sprinkle with cumin, chilli flakes, pepper and salt.
5. Knead the lentil mixture for 5-10 minutes. Shape into lengths the size of a thumb or make balls.
6. Place endive leaves on a dish and the lentil köfte on top of them. Serve at room temperature.

Kadin budu köfte

Women's thighs (minced meat)

750g (26.4oz) lean veal mince • 3 tbsp rice, washed • 200ml (6.8 fl.oz) water • 2 onions, grated • 150ml (5.1fl.oz) olive oil • 6 twigs parsley, leaves and stems separated • 3 eggs, 2 of which are whisked • 3-4 tbsp bread crumbs • cumin powder • pepper and salt

1 Cook the rice with the water until all the liquid is absorbed. Set aside.
2 In the meantime glaze the onions in some oil and add the parsley stems with half of the minced meat.
3 Wait until all the liquid from the meat has been absorbed. Remove the pan from the hob.
4 Add the contents of the pan to the raw minced meat in a separate dish. Add the whole egg and the rest of the parsley. Sprinkle to taste with cumin, pepper and salt.
5 Knead for 5 minutes, then mix the rice through it. Shape into oval pieces the size of an egg.
6 Roll each piece through the whisked eggs and after that through the bread crumbs. Fry the minced meat in hot oil on a high flame until it is done and serve directly.

THIGHS This dish is named 'women's thighs' due the oval shape of the pieces and thankfully not the type of meat used to make it..

Baklava

Walnut cake

500g (1.10 lbs) flour • 1½ tsp salt • 1 tbsp olive oil • 4 tsp lemon juice • 2 eggs • 2-3 tbsp lukewarm water • 100g (3.52oz) corn flour mixed with 100g (3.52oz) flour • 250g (8.81oz) butter, melted • 100g (3.52oz) walnuts, peeled and pressed • 100g (3.52oz) pistachio nuts, minced • 2 tbsp pistachio nuts, for garnishing • For the syrup: 1kg (2.2lbs) sugar • 600ml (20.3fl.oz) water • 2 tbsp lemon juice

1   Make a hole in the flour and add the salt, the oil, the lemon juice and the eggs.
2   Knead well and add the water drop by drop until it is completely absorbed.
3   Knead for another 5-10 minutes. Then leave the dough to rest for 15 minutes under a moist towel.
4   Knead again briefly. Make into balls the size of an egg. Roll through the corn flour and leave to rest under a moist towel.
5   With a rolling pin make slices with a diameter of 15 cm. Sprinkle with extra corn flour when the dough sticks to the rolling pin.
6   Put the slices on top of each other. Sprinkle after every 3rd slice with melted butter. Leave them to rest for 1 hour under a moist towel.
7   Preheat the oven to 180°C (350F, Gas 4). Take only 1 slice from the pile each time and roll it out so that it is a 1½mm thick patch the size of a form you used. Sprinkle every patch with drops of melted butter.
8   Grease a heat resistant dish and put the patches of dough in it. Sprinkle some walnuts and minced pistachio nuts on to every 3rd layer. Use the entirety of the remaining nuts on the second-last layer.
9   Cut diamond shapes into the surface of the dough. Smear with the rest of the butter. Bake in the oven in about 45 minutes until it is golden brown.
10 Make the syrup by cooking the sugar for 5 minutes in the water. Add the lemon juice and leave to boil for 1 minute.
11 Allow syrup to cool. When Baklava comes out of the oven, pour the syrup over it.
12 Cover and allow to cool. Garnish with pistachio nuts.

TIP: Serve baklava with tea or with ice cream as dessert. Buy it fresh from a bakery that makes it on site. During the sugar feast fresh baklava is available everywhere. The most famous bakers come from the Gaziantep-area and the creamy filling they make is especially sought after.

Kayısı tatlısı

Filled apricots with cream and pistachio nuts

200g (7.05oz) dried apricots, without pips • 325ml (11fl.oz) water • 4 tbsp sugar • juice of ½ lemon • 1 tbsp grated lemon peel • kaymak, or fresh cream • 100g (3.52oz) unsalted pistachio nuts, chopped

1   Soak the apricots for 4 hours in the water. Remove the apricots and set the water aside.
2   Add the sugar, the lemon juice and the lemon peel to the water.
3   Bring to boil and leave to cook for a few minutes. Turn the heat down and add the apricots. Leave them to simmer on a low heat for 25 minutes.
4   Leave the fruit to cool in the syrup. Then cut the apricots carefully open lengthwise without cutting them completely through and fill them with the kaymak.
5   Serve on a dish. Pour a thin layer of syrup on top and sprinkle with the pistachio nuts.

Aşure

Cold fruit soup

500g (1.10 lbs) asurelik bugday (oval wheat crumbs) • 50g (1.76oz) orange peel, finely cut • 1.5l (50.7 water • 100ml (3.4fl.oz) milk • 1 tbsp corn flour • 100g (3.52oz) chickpeas, soaked for 8 hours • 100g (3.52oz) white beans, soaked for 8 hours • 1 tsp salt • 750g (26.4oz) sugar • 50g (1.76oz) yellow raisins, soaked for 8 hours • 5 fresh figs, in pieces (if dried you should soak them first) • 5 fresh apricots, in pieces (if dried you should soak them first) • 200g (7.05oz) whole hazelnuts and walnuts, peeled • 1 tsp cinnamon powder • 100ml (3.4fl.oz) rose water

NOAH This soup is a traditional dessert, that, according to legend, was made for the first time on the Arc of Noah. Aşure is eaten every year after the twelve day fast period on the Alevitic holiday. Nowadays the cold soup is appearing on more and more menu cards of restaurants.

1   Gently boil the bugday with the orange peel in water and leave to simmer for 4 hours.
2   After that, mix the milk with the corn flour and add to the bugday.
3   Add the chickpeas, white beans and salt and boil for another hour.
4   Add the sugar and boil for another 30 minutes.
5   Add the raisins, figs, apricots, nuts and cinnamon and leave to simmer for another 10 minutes.
6   Take the pan from the hob. Stir the rose water through the soup.
7   Leave covered until the soup thickens (about 30 minutes). Serve cooled in soup plates.

Kanlı portakal helvası

Blood orange dessert

500ml (17fl.oz) juice of blood oranges, or pink grapefruits •
2 tbsp sugar • 1 cinnamon stick • 4 tbsp rice flour • 75g (2.64oz)
pistachio nuts, chopped

SPECIAL Apart from the famous blocks of helva made from sweetened sesame paste, helvas are also made from semolina, rice flour, butter or milk. This traditional recipe is only used for special occasions, such as remembrance days for family members.

1   Bring $2/3$ of the juice to the boil with the sugar and the cinnamon stick.
2   Take the pan of the heat and leave to soak in for 10 minutes, then remove the cinnamon stick.
3   In the meantime mix the leftover juice with the rice flour. Add this to the cooked juice and slowly bring to the boil again while constantly stirring. Serve with the pistachio nuts. It is delicious both warm and cold.

Sultan kokteyl

Sultan's cocktail

325ml (11fl.oz) dry vermouth • 325ml (11fl.oz) gin • 325ml (11fl.oz) freshly squeezed orange juice, sieved • ice cubes

1   Shake all ingredients well in a cocktail shaker.
2   Sieve the cocktail and pour it into 4 glasses.

Uludağ kokteyl

Cocktail from Uludağ

325ml (11fl.oz) cognac • 325ml (11fl.oz) lemon peel • 325ml (11fl.oz) mint liqueur • ice cubes

1 Shake all ingredients well in a cocktail shaker.
2 Sieve the cocktail and pour it into 4 glasses. Garnish with mint leaves.

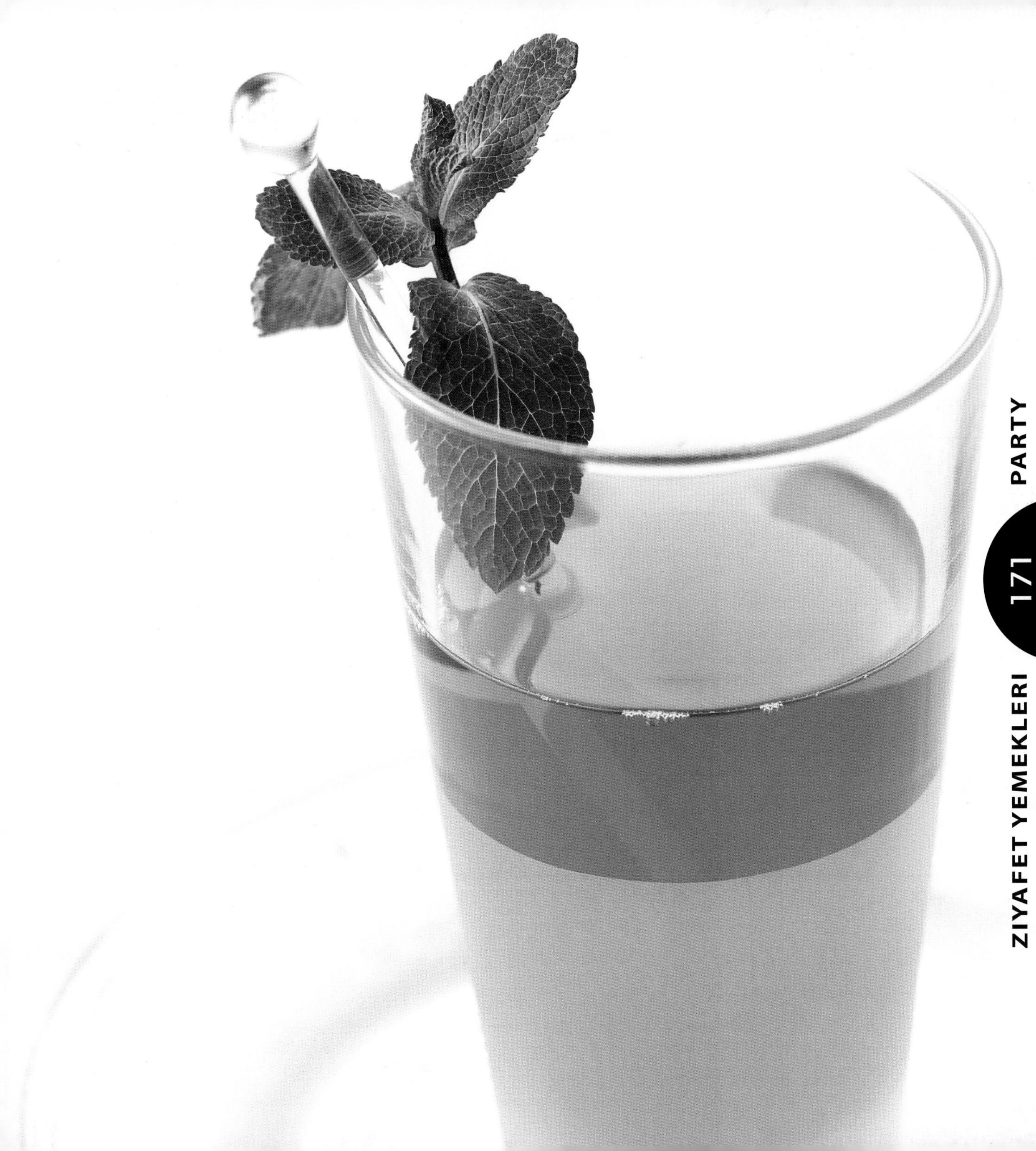

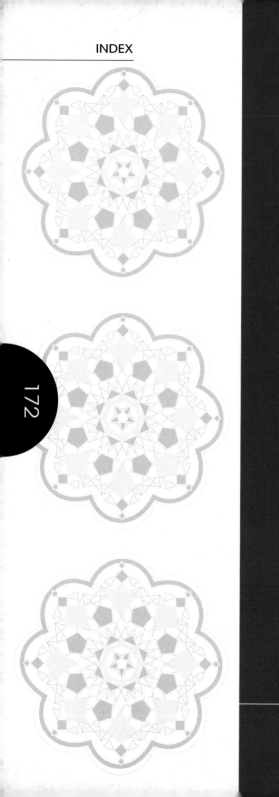

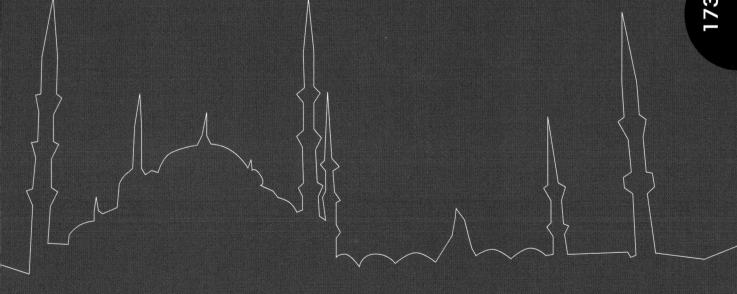

INDEX

INDEX